I Forgive Me:

Your 31-day Guide to Self - forgiveness, Internal Release and Spiritual Restoration

Whom the Son sets free is FREE indeed

Tabitha L. McClarity

ISBN 13: 978-1-7334426-0-2

ISBN 10: 1-7334426-0-X

PRINTED IN THE UNITED STATES OF AMERICA

Please look for these Titles by Tabitha L. McClarity

The 9 C.L.E.A.R. V.I.E.W.™ Tips for Powerful Life Transformations:

9 Simple Steps for achieving powerful life transformations and have your best life NOW!!

For more information about this Author, Speaker, Life/Success Coach visit us on the web

www.tabithamcclarity.com

www.iforgivemetm.com

770-344-8733

Tabitha@tabithamcclarity.com

info@tabithamclarity.com

FB: Tabitha Rowland McClarity

Instagram: @tabitha_macicu

Acknowledgments

To God, this book is balm for the soul. Thank you for giving the awe-inspiring word to transform the lives of your people. To help them to receive your forgiveness, your loving kindness and your peace. Thank you for opening my heart, my eyes, my mouth and my mind. I pray that you are pleased with me. To Randy, Husband and best friend, I love you, thank you for our journey together, these past five years have taught me tremendous faith, patience and trust. To My Children & Grandchildren, Chris, Shay, Deana, DeVante, Quindarious, D'Aja, Peyton, Azayla, DeVonte Jr.,

Bentlei, Damian Jr. & Deklynn—you are my focus; I love you! To my parents Jerry & Ruby Rowland...I am so blessed to have you as my main role models...I love you. Thank you for always being there for me. To my Siblings Carmen, Jerry, Melissa, Tara, Sterling, Micah & Courtney, you mean the world to me, I love you!!! To all my nieces & nephews...Auntie Lynne Loves you.

Table of Contents

Preface

WOW, it was a cold Fall morning and my week had been a whirlwind. President Obama had just been re-elected and people (Democrats and Republicans) were trying to recover from the hardest fought political campaign ever!!! That was in 2012 or so I thought! Then 2016 proved to be an even more hard-fought campaign as Donald Trump was elected. It was amazing how the emotional toll of these elections had devastated the nation and the world. Anyway, this is not a political book, but it sets the atmosphere for the time we are in and it is part of the "right now".

As I sat there at my desk, I felt overwhelmed and compelled to get this book out to you. God said...YOU HAVE TO START THIS TODAY and I responded OK (Lord, I am doing better at listening to your still small voice). It was like the words were over-flowing in my brain and I could not focus on anything else but getting this information on the page. So here it goes.

Over the last year or so I have been really focusing on starting my Life Coaching/ Business Consulting Company. I have received my Coaching Certification; I have been reading books, visiting other Coaches websites, hosting New Entrepreneur classes, giving free coaching sessions etc. I mean you name it, as it relates to Life coaching, I have been trying to submerge myself in it in order to hone my skills. I come alive, when I am facilitating the transformation of a person who wants to see AWESOME things happen in their lives.

I have always had a passion for helping people and encouraging them to see the best in themselves. That's how God made me and to be honest, that is why he made me. I understand that now. As I was saying, I have been working diligently on perfecting my gift so that I could reach the masses and facilitate transformations for people who want to make a positive change for their life and/or businesses. One day as I was sitting in front of the computer working on the title of what was to be my first book, I prayed that the book would change people's lives and help them become free from burdens and dream killers. In that moment God spoke to my spirit and the conversation that we were having was about how people would benefit from the book. My question was, "What could I put in the book that would encourage and empower others?" The answer became clear to me that people were not ready for another empowerment book, because they could not "Receive" empowerment. There were some things that were blocking their blessing receptors and causing them not to operate in courage and power. As I questioned God about this, He shared with me the that most people cannot receive His blessings because they are burdened down by unforgiveness, not the unforgiveness of others, but ***They have not forgiven themselves.*** *When this dropped in my spirit it was like time stopped and I had what my Friend Karessa calls an "Ah Ha" moment. I* *mean really look at your life right now. From the time that we could communicate it was instilled in us to share, to be kind to others, to love others, to do things for others, to give things to others, to forgive others, to be a team player, to make decisions or collaborations with others etc., etc., etc. There was so much focus on not being selfish and self-centered, our society forgot to balance the persona with self-awareness and self-appreciation. So here we are today. People are not balanced.*

So, Tabitha what do you mean "Not balanced"? Ok I am going to ask you three questions and as you answer them you are going to be able to see what I mean. I really want you to pause right here and spend some time thinking about these questions. This book is not intended to be read like a love story or a quick novel its intended to be read, soaked in, meditated on, activated (that means YOU TAKE ACTION), and results driven. Don't short yourself, you've been doing that for far too long already.

#1. How often do you spent time meditating or just by yourself; saying how wonderful you are, how beautiful you are, how caring you are?

*Answer:*________________________

____

____

____

____

____

____

#2. How many times have you put someone else's needs above your own? (Remember I am not talking about being selfish I am talking about being balanced and/or self-aware-we will talk about this more later).

*Answer:*______________________________

____

____

____

____

____

#3. How many times have you thought that you were not deserving (worthy) or turned down a gift/recognition that someone was trying to give you? (This one is often coupled with you telling people...You didn't have to do that...YES, THEY DID because you deserved it)

*Answer:*________________________

____

____

____

____

As I was saying; years and years of being out of balance with unforgiveness for yourself has left you unable to really experience your blessing and your destiny as God intended for you/for US to experience them. Your "Blessing Receptors" are out of whack. You have forgiven everyone else and set them free to be blessed abundantly.

I am sure sometimes you look at those same people and say "Since we let the nonsense go, Sister Mary know she is flourishing, God I am thankful for you blessing HER, but I don't see you moving for me right now. Well guess what, maybe you asked her to forgive you and she did, but at the same time you did not ask YOU to FORGIVE you ...Huh? Again, your blessing receptors are blocked. See let me paint a picture for you.

In the body there are millions and millions of sending and receiving nerves that tells the body how to function properly. The sender tells the receptor what is going on and the receptor communicates with brain and then the brain communicates with you. Whether it is vision, taste, touch, smell or hearing there must be some receiving nerves for your body to function and operate properly. If there is something in your body that is out of whack and the communication from the sender nerves and the receiving nerves are blocked, then your receptors cannot get the message that your senders are trying to give you. The same thing applies to us in the Spirit as it relates to unforgiveness. If we are one sided (Have our Focus on others ALLLLL the time) then we cannot receive when God is sending something especially for us. We misinterpret His blessings and often give them back or pass them to someone else simply because unforgiveness (self-unforgiveness has blocked out the feelings of self-worth in God).

To me self-unforgiveness can be harsher on you because you are constantly speaking negativity to yourself about how you don't deserve to be blessed. If God delays your prayer, self-unforgiveness will come in and say "You know God is not going to do that for you because you did so and so...Does this sound familiar?

As you read this book. I don't want you to think about anyone else. You have my **permission** *to think about you. To focus on healing you, to focus on unblocking your "blessing receptors". In the book I will talk about several personal experiences and experiences that I have witnessed. I will use Biblical scriptures and other resources to usher you into* *your own self- forgiveness. We are going to take a 31-day journey and I invite you to be fully engaged, to expect change, to embrace the change and to look forward to becoming balanced in your Love and Care for others as well as your Love and Care for yourself. It's time for the restoral you have been waiting on and missing! I know our Father is waiting there with open arms. The main scripture for this book comes from* ***Matthew 6:14 (NIV) For if you forgive men when they sin against you, your Heavenly Father***

will also forgive you. *This scripture says" forgive men" this means all men and women including yourself. As you read this book. I don't want you to think about anyone else. Again, you have my* ***permission*** *to think about you. To focus on healing you, to focus on re-building your "blessing receptors". As a matter of fact, YOU HAVE GOD'S PERMISSION.*

Once you have spoken the "Lord, I forgive me" for that day, do exactly that... FORGIVE YOURSELF and move forward; you have allowed the enemy (the illusion) to use things against you way too long. I hope this book blesses you as much as it has blessed me.

Oh, I almost forgot, throughout the book, you will see what I call "Sidebars". In a court of law, a "Sidebar" is a side conversation between the Judge and both the Prosecuting and Defense Attorneys. I've seen this only in the movies, but what happens is the Judge would call the Attorneys either to his bench or chambers to have a side conversation

which most of the time would be pertaining to an argument of law. In the movies, the audience gets to hear the side bar, but the awaiting court room does not. In this book you will get to read the "Sidebars". The "Sidebar" may be conversation between God and I that I let you in on, a Prayer, or even additional instructions after a Chapter.

In addition to this book I have also created supplemental resources designed to give you a call to action. Please take advantage of these resources.

Prayer

Lord I ask right now that you let your spirit fall fresh on me. Help me to forgive myself and be set free from anything that is causing me not to receive the blessings you have for me. I ask that you forgive me of all of my sins and wash me white as snow. I understand that I am only made worthy because of You and the precious Blood of Jesus. I know that You Love me and want what is best for me. Lord help me to be balanced in my Love and Care for others as well as the Love and Care for myself. Today I walk in your restorative power. I want to live in your "DEVINE" will. In Jesus name – Amen

Intention

Lord it my intention that every reader of this book is restored to you and that your MIGHTY POWER moves in every area of their lives. It is my intention that people are restored wholly Spiritually, Mentally, Physically and Financially; NOTHING MISSING, AND NOTHING BROKEN. It is my intention that You get the glory out of the blessings that the readers of this book WILL experience. Lord, it is my intention that this book is purchased, disseminated, taught and lived by millions of people worldwide in every language. In Jesus Name

Matthew 6:14 (NIV) For if you forgive men when they sin against you, your Heavenly Father will also forgive you.

This scripture says" forgive men" this means all men and women........................including yourself.

Day One: I forgive me for not being committed

Day One: I forgive me for not being committed. Lord today I forgive me for not being committed to the things that you have called me to.

God created you for a specific reason, of course we know it is to worship Him, but I am also talking about your functions in the Earth that manifest His likeness to others. God has called you to be His child first of all, but among many things He has also created you to be a good son/daughter to your Earthly parents, a good husband/wife to your spouse, a good Father/Mother to your children, a good brother/sister to your siblings a good friend, a good worker, a co-worker etc. etc. etc. With all of these things comes great responsibility and commitment. The issue is that sometimes we have not been committed to functioning in these roles as we should. I mean do not get me wrong, I know that wearing all these hats can be over whelming, but I am not talking about that. I am talking about the times that we intentionally are slow to fulfill our commitments to others. I'll give you an example. Sometimes you are not as committed on your job as you should be. It is even harder when it is a job that you do not like!!!

I remember a time when I went through a rough patch at work. It started about two years into my becoming a first line Supervisor. I felt like I was doing a great job, but I consistently kept getting feedback, that I needed to build relationships and get out of my office more. I did not agree with the feedback and really felt like I was being singled out. Because I had this perception, my behavior begins to change negatively, I stopped participating in meetings, became very withdrawn and empathetic towards my work. I mean I did the work, but I was not committed to the work. I did what I needed to do to keep a job. It had gotten so bad that even when I pulled up to the gate to go to work, I could feel my personally transform into a mean and defensive me. It was like I went to work prepared to fight, prepared to complain and prepared to look for the worst in people because that was what I felt they were doing to me. Every day I went to work acting this way then on Sundays I would wave holy hands and send up fake praise to God. I say that this was fake praise because there is no way that anyone could have that much anger and distain in their heart and be able to truly praise God. Darkness and light cannot be on at the same time. Anyway, I will never forget this, it was around review time and I had made up in my mind that I was going to have a heart-to heart conversation with my manager and ask her why I was being singled out and treated the way that I was. In my mind, I was going to set things straight with her. Well the meeting started and I was ready to start throwing my fiery darts at my Manager (of course I was going to do this in a way that would get my point across and not get me FIRED). So, as we began to talk, she allowed me to get all of my anger out and then asked me.... very calmly I might add, why I felt this way? Then when I told her she politely, gave me examples of how I used to act and how I was acting then, she reminded me of why she hired me and politely told me that I was no longer that person...As I began to see myself. I cried. She didn't say a word. YES, this happened at work.

At that moment I realized I had lost focus; that I had lost the spirit of commitment that I so loved having, that I had lost the spirit of Excellence. Not for serving man but for serving God. I remember her asking what can I do to help you get back to the old Tab? At that point the conversation changed I change. We developed a plan to get me back on track. I had to get out of the ditch. And I did. What our conversation reminded me of was that I was not on the job to please the people I was there to please God and He was not pleased with my actions or behavior towards His people (Even when people are not serving God they still his people) My commitment to my job was restored and I was able to flourish because of it. The key was that I acknowledged that I had not been committed to my job I asked God to forgive me and I forgave myself and made a 180 degree turn around. Maybe you are committed to your job like you are supposed to be, but not to your spouse. Maybe you are committed to your spouse, but not your children. Whatever it is, now is the time to look at where you are not committed and make the change. Say out loud, I have not been committed to ______. Lord please forgive me. Then say to yourself. I forgive me for not being committed to __________. How did that feel? It is totally different from saying to someone else. I forgive you for not being committed to ____, right? There is a song by Walter Hawkins called "Fully Committed" and I am reminded of the part of the lyrics that says "All that I am and all that I hope to be. All of my desires and all of my abilities. You see I'm fully committed to your will and to your way. I'll make the sacrifice to do what you ask of me. My Love's forever and Jesus you're all that I need, and I could never repay what you did just for me. I give my life fully committed to you. It is finished, move forward and receive the blessing. You have an opportunity today to be fully committed to God and everything that He has called you to.

Internal Release: *Breathe in and out 5 times slowly and repeat aloud in the mirror: "I release the burden that the lack of commitment has weighed on me. I am complete and restored and I am ready to face the day!"*

Declaration of Spiritual Restoration

Prayer: *Lord thank you for renewing your fresh spirit in me. Thank you for reviving my commitment to you, to my responsibilities and to everything you have created me to be the steward of. Give me a fresh anointing to remain committed right now in Jesus name. Amen.*

Sidebar: Before we move to the next chapter. I want to let you know that I am a HUGE fan of journaling. In every book that I write I will always ask you to meditate on what you have read and journal what you are thinking. Take time to write some things down on each day. Also, just because the book is written in a 31-day format does not mean you have to finish it in 31 days. Take your time, you may need to let some of these things marinate… don't let them cling to you.

John 8:36 Whom the Son sets free is free indeed

If you have the workbook; at this time, please complete the exercises for today.

Day Two: I forgive me for Lying

Day Two: Lord today I forgive me for lying. OOOUUUCCCHHH. There is no one on Earth who has not told a lie. Oh, I am sure that some of you reading this book right now are saying "Huh, honey I don't tell lies. I'm straight up, whatever comes up come out" That statement within itself is a LIE. Think about it. Here is what the Bible says about lying:

Proverbs 6:16-19 (NET)

There are six things that the Lord hates, even seven things that are an abomination to Him haughty eyes, a lying tongue, and hands that shed innocent blood, a heart that devises wicked plans, feet that are swift to run to evil, a false witness who pours out lies and a person who spreads discord among family members.

That's deep. Just think about it, how many of us know people who tell lies, just to be telling them. They don't mean any harm in doing it and sometimes the lies just jump out before they have an opportunity to stop them. Just think about how quick they come up. I knew this lady once who just lied for no apparent reason. You could say hello to her and she would ask a question like "How was your day?" and by the time you answered and told her what was going on she had a lie that almost matched exactly to what you had been going through. For quite some time this bothered me to no end. So much so that I just quit talking to her at all because I did not want to make her lie to me about anything. What happen out of this experience is that I was more aware of when half-truths (lies) would come out of my own mouth. I had to start rebuking myself and asking God to give me the proper words to say. No, I do not tell malicious lies, but I don't always tell the truth either and sadly the opposite of the truth is what? A LIE. The thing about it is the scripture did not classify levels or lies or excusable lies, but we do. How many times have you told a little lie to protect someone's feelings? How many times have you told a lie to protect yourselves? This one is rough isn't it? No one wants to be a liar even when we have the best of intentions. Are you sitting there trying to justify why or when it is ok to lie? I'm sure some of you are saying, what if it is to save someone's feelings? Ok, if that is the case then maybe your approach could be to say to the person "That question puts me in a bad position, because if I answer truthfully, it is going to hurt your feelings and I don't want to do that. So instead of lying I will keep this to myself. Or do you really want to know?" You could also use the instructions from your childhood when the older people would say "If you do not have anything good to say, don't say anything at all." Lying is rough because depending upon the situation, people can always justify why they do it. Justifying a lie never makes it right, but it is what we do. Lord Jesus, I forgive me for lying, I know that telling a lie is something that you hate and I no longer want to do it. Please give me the right words to say even in the worst of circumstance where it would be easier to tell a little "white" lie. Help me to do the right things so that I do not have to lie. And when I find myself in a bad situation, please let the truth prevail. Help me to realize that you are the way the truth and the life and the only way that I can get to you is by operating in the truth.

Internal Release: *Breathe in and out 5 times slowly and repeat aloud in the mirror: I am delivered from a lying tongue. I no longer have the need to say or believe things that are not true.*

Declaration of Spiritual Restoral

Prayer: *Thank you for helping me to be honest when I speak. Thank you for giving me the right words to say and thank you for helping me to not say anything if lying is my only alternative. In Jesus name, amen.*

Sidebar: I'm going to put this right here so that you will understand who you are dealing with going forward. God knows ALLL about me. He knows all of my flaws, so I have nothing to hide from you. I promise to be transparent to you because God has blessed me to be able to do so. Hopefully through my truths you will be able to verbalize yours (however good or bad they may be), forgive yourself and receive the blessings that you SOOOO richly deserve. The Christian thing to do would be to tell you to go back and correct all of your lies, but to be honest, I have told so many I wouldn't even know where to start or who to start with.

So how could I expect you to do that? The best we can do from today forward is acknowledge the flaw, ask for sincere forgiveness and then forgive yourself.

Lie Quiz

Name the top five things you have lied about.
Then resolve to stop!!

1. ______________________________

____

2. ______________________________

____

3. ______________________________

____

4. ______________________________

____

5. ______________________________

____

Proverbs 6:16-19 (NET)

16 There are six things that
the Lord hates, even seven
things that are an
abomination to Him 17
haughty eyes, a lying
tongue, and hands that shed
innocent blood, 18 a heart
that devises wicked plans,

feet that are swift to run to evil, *19* ***a false witness who pours out lies and a person who spreads discord among family members.***

If you have the workbook; at this time, please complete the exercises for today.

Day Three: I forgive me for thinking I was not worthy of being blessed

Day three: I forgive me for not thinking I was worthy of being blessed. WOOAAHHHH Did I just say that? Yessss I did. Saved Tabitha that thinks you can just pray, and God shows up and shows out.... well really sometimes it does not happen like that. And the enemy uses that as a trick of defeat. So many times

I have prayed and believed whole heartedly that God was going to move a certain way and when His answer was either "No" or not right now, I ended up being dejected or HIGHLY disappointed. I would always think that God said no because I was not worthy or because I had done so much wrong that he was not going to let me have any blessings until I paid for all the wrong, I have done. I didn't really grasp what the word said about God's forgiveness for me. I mean just listen to this.

Psalm 103

1 Praise the LORD, my soul; all my inmost being, praise his holy name. 2 Praise the LORD, my soul,

and forget not all his benefits—3 who forgives all your sins and heals all your diseases, 4 who redeems your life from the pit and crowns you with love and compassion, 5 who satisfies your desires with good things so that your youth is renewed like the eagle's. 6 The LORD works righteousness and justice for all the oppressed. 7 He made known his ways to Moses, his deeds to the people of Israel: 8 The LORD is compassionate and gracious, slow to anger, abounding in love. 9 He will not always accuse, nor will he harbor his anger forever; [10] he does not treat us as our sins deserve or repay us according to our iniquities. [11] For as high as the heavens are above the earth, so great is his love for those who fear him; ***[12] as far as the east is from the west, so far as he removed our transgressions from us.*** *[13] As a father has compassion on his children, so the LORD has compassion on those who fear him; [14] for he knows how we are formed, he remembers that we are dust. [15] The life of mortals is like grass, they flourish like a flower of the field; [16] the wind blows over it and it is gone, and its place remembers it no more. [17] But from everlasting to everlasting the LORD's love is with those who fear* *him, and his righteousness with their children's children—[18] with those who keep his covenant and remember to obey his precepts.[19] The LORD has established his throne in heaven, and his kingdom rules over all. [20] Praise the LORD, you his angels, you mighty ones who do his bidding, who obey his word. [21] Praise the LORD, all his heavenly hosts, you his servants who do his will. 22 Praise the Lord, all his works everywhere in his dominion. Praise the Lord, my soul.*

DID you get that? As far as the East is from the West!! So, let's do a little physics...the East and the West NEVER touch they go to infinity so that means God forgives you to infinity!! HE NEVER ALLOWS THE GUILT OF SIN TO TOUCH US AGAIN ONCE WE ASK HIM FOR FORGIVENESS. We are the ones that expect "payback", so we think that every delay in a prayer, or even a block in a prayer, or a no to a prayer is punishment for something we did in the past. When that is absolutely not true!

I've been an entrepreneur for most of my life. I started a Tax business around 2004 and have worked during tax season for the last 13 years and have has good success with it, but what I realized is that it took my time from the Lord. As I continued to pray for it to prosper, I kept running into brick walks. Sometimes I would do 200 clients or 300 hundred clients, but it was never enough to get to level to be able to leave my job. For the longest I wondered why the Lord was not listening to my cry about this, but as I was writing this book, I realized that I was taking time from the Lord. I mean I already had a full-time job that was pressing me plus being a wife plus working during tax season. I kept putting God on the back burner. I wanted to leave my job so bad, but I couldn't when the tax office was not bringing in the income that would replace what I would be leaving and that included my six-figure base salary, plus annual bonus, and benefits. AS bad as I wanted to leave I couldn't I prayed so hard for years and even felt like God had given me the permission to leave, but the fear of failure grappled me and I did not leave I wanted to see the profits before letting go. I didn't feel like I was worthy to the Lord to bless me if I stepped out. I had had so many small defeats that I couldn't step out on a big something that would be an extraordinary victory. That ending up being a cycle with my Beauty Supply business and both of my daycares. I kept falling short and could not make them be the success I wanted them to be. I kept finding myself saying Lord why can't I be successful in these businesses and I had to realize my expectation for failure, the thought that was pre-set in my spirit saying that I was not worthy to be blessed was my own blessing blockers!! Do you have some of those same self-defeating actions and thoughts today? I encourage you to STOP them right now. God has forgiven you, now you have to forgive you!!!

Internal Release: *Breathe in and out 5 times slowly and repeat aloud in the mirror: I am WORTHY TO BE BLESSED. My Heavenly Father loves me and wants to bless me!*

Declaration of Spiritual Restoral: *Lord I forgive me for not thinking I am worthy to receive your blessings, your elevation, your promotion, your success. I know that you sent your son Jesus to pay a price for me to live victorious and I accept that today. I am not worthy because of me, but I am worthy because of you and I thank you for my blessings!!*

Psalm 103:12:

as far as the east
is from the
west, so far as he
removed our
transgressions
from us.

If you have the workbook; at this time, please complete the exercises for today.

Day Four: I forgive me for procrastinating

Day Four: I forgive me for procrastinating. Wow procrastination is my middle name!! I wonder how many opportunities I have missed because I didn't move when I was supposed to?
Lord today I forgive me for operating in the spirit of procrastination.
I don't know if I've already mentioned this to you all or not but when God speaks to me, he calls me Lynne so when I talk about him speaking to me I will always say "God said Lynne".
If I had a dollar for every time God said Lynne do this or do that, I know I would be a millionaire. What about you? I

mean how many times have you been nudged in the spirit or in your heart or in you mind to do a certain thing and you say..." I'll do it tomorrow" but tomorrow never comes.

Procrastination is actions that can cause blessings to be delayed and denied.

The WordNet dictionary defines procrastination as the act of putting off or delaying or deferring an action to a later time. The key component of this definition is the portion of the definition that states "to a later time". I hate to be the barer of bad news, but we don't have a lot of time to be in the habit of delaying anything.

For me procrastination is a combination of laziness, (yep I said it) and fear.

Lazy Procrastination, now that is a combination of words for you but in reality, we all have participated in being lazy and slow about putting off important things for a later time. Just imagine the break throughs, opportunities and blessings that we have missed because we were too lazy and have not acted until it is too late. People often use the saying what God has for me is for me and that very well may be true, but the window of opportunity does not stay open forever. Procrastination causes stagnation and stagnation can cause death to your dreams.

I will tell you a story. I live in the small town in Dallas, everyday on my route to work I pass a daycare building that has been vacated for about three years. Everyday I pass it God said "Lynne go see about getting that building" Well one day about 2 years ago I did contact the company and the Agent shared with me that it was a booming business that had been closed due to the previous owner having some issues after the death of her husband. The building was big and still had ALL of the furniture still in it. I had owned two daycares (you will hear more about them later) in the past and loved running the businesses and I was very interested in getting back into it. The Agent told me the banks asking price and I was like ok thank you (really high). The building stayed vacant for another year and I *glanced at it everyday saying to myself "if that building is still open tomorrow, I am going to call the bank and make an offer. I never did I kept procrastinating. Then around the beginning of May 2019 the Lord said "Lynne fax an offer of $250,000.00 (which was like 3 times less than what they wanted) into the Agent tell them you want to enter into a lease to purchase option with no money down and paying them $500 per month for one year in order to give you time to get your credit restored in order to get the business loan. Explain to them that it takes 90-180 days for a facility to be their license approved by the state of Georgia and if the business is going to be successful you would need the remaining* *six to nine months to build the business. When God said this to me, I was like HAHAHA yeah right like the bank is going to go for that, but ok I will do it.*

You think I did it? NOPE I drove by the building Monday through Friday for the next four weeks playing the scenario over and over again in my mind and hearing God say "Lynne fax the agent an offer for $250,000" I kept saying I'm going to do it tomorrow. TOMORROW NEVER CAME. On May 30, 2019 in my normal route to work, I passed the same building as I always do, but I noticed that the Realtor sign was gone. The way that the building sits off of the road there are trees in front of it so you really can't see it, but I just knew. I *turned around and pulled into the parking lot and guess what, the sign was gone and there was a cleaning van and another car there. My heart sank because I knew I had missed the opportunity.... Procrastination = Disobedience = MISSED BLESSING. EHM EHM EHM THAT'S STINGING ME RIGHT NOW*

Internal Release: *Breathe in and out 5 times slowly and repeat aloud in the mirror: I am about my Father's business I have to many gifts and talents to be slothful in my actions.*

Declaration of Spiritual Restoral: *Lord Thank you for helping me not to procrastinate when I hear your voice. I will move when you say move. I am grateful for your love and care towards me that allows me to have love and care towards myself. Thank you for helping me to understand that you are not required to bless me but that you bless me because you love me. I will act at the right time so be prepared for the overflow. In Jesus name, amen.*

PROCRASTINATION =

DISOBEDIANCE =

MISSED BLESSING

People often use the saying what God has for me is for me and that very well may be true, but the window of opportunity does not stay open forever.

May 30, 2019

Tabitha Rowland McClarity is feeling heartbroken.
May 30 at 10:02 AM

I had a very humbling experience this morning God told me to move on something and I did not do it so now that window of opportunity is closed all I have to say to you this morning IS TAKE ACTION & Move when God tells you to move You won't know if you will fail or succeed if you never try

Nichelle Ford Thank you I need see this
Love · Reply · 1w 1

Diane Damond Amen but take courage you will have a second chance
Like · Reply · 1w

Tabitha Rowland McClarity Diane Damond TY but not for this I won't
Like · Reply · 1w

Diane Damond So sorry
Like · Reply · 1w

Tabitha Rowland McClarity Diane Damond no worries this was a lesson for me I'm fine wasn't nothing hurt but my pride I talked myself out of a blessing b/c I was focusing on failing!!! I kept saying I will do it tomorrow but I didn't n someone else did! GOD IS GOOD
Like · Reply · 1w

Write a reply...

Diane Damond Amen
Like · Reply · 1w

Shavonda Johnson Pennymon Yes yes and yes!!! I made a post earlier and now I just seen yours. This was confirmation.
Like · Reply · 1w

If you have the workbook; at this time, please complete the exercises for today.

Day Five: I forgive me for not being a good money manager

Day Five: I forgive me for not being a good money manager. Man, I wish I could use the emoji eyeballs on this one. MONEY MONEY MONEY where did you go? Over my lifetime I know that I have made well over a million dollars. Since my early thirties I've worked and ran my small tax business. I easily made $150,000.00 to $200,000 annually but for the life of me I cannot tell you where that money is. I spent thousands on clothes and shoes. I made sure my children were provided for financially. I paid bills. I started businesses that were *money pits. I loaned people money. I gave people money. I paid for training to increase my skills in other things that I wanted to learn, but none of it has made me wealthy at all. See I've made money, but I have not been a good steward or manager of my money. Even as I am sitting here thinking about what to write I am like gguurrlll you have really messed up some bags in your day. It's ok though because today is my day of redemption and today is the day that I forgive me for all of that!! And today is the day that you forgive yourself for the same thing!*

Being a good money manager simply means that you do the right thing with the finances that you are given. I know some of you may be looking at this *part like "What?!?! What do you mean what I am given shoot I only make $20,000 a year?" Yeah, I know and once you are a good manager of the $20,000 doors will open to allow you to get to $30,000, $40,000, $50,000 and so on.*

My first job was when I was about 15 at the Dairy Queen, then again when I was 17, I worked at Del Taco in Cedartown. When I turned 18, I worked fulltime from until now. In my early twenties I worked 70-80 hours per week at a bakery and brought home a good check. My issue was I would take that check ad buy non-sense instead of paying my bills. If I was going to the club, I bought a new "man trap" outfit so I would look like a million bucks when I *barely had $10. When it was time to pay my bills, I did not have the money and would have to run to my parents to bail me out. That cycle worked for years, all I had to do was to go to them with tears and they would always come through. Then one day, I don't know what it was, well yes, I do it was the Lord, but nevertheless, I was at my normal routine of working, spending my money on non-sense then calling my Mama and Daddy for a bail out. This time my Mama said no. I was like wwhhhaaatttt ohh mmyy GGOODDDD what am I going to do. They are going to cut my lights off TOMORROW and my old faithful parents have said no. Now you are talking about panic mode and tears, but Mama and*

Daddy didn't budge and yes, my lights got turned off. I had to wait until I got my check to get them back on.

You would think after being either left in the dark, or in the cold, or bathing with cold water or being served eviction notices I would learn to do better with my money, but I didn't.

I know you might be saying didn't your parents teach you how to pay bills? No, they didn't. Mama mainly handled the money and I don't ever remember the lights, gas, or water ever being turned off. I just remember her saying, you got to pay your bills on time. That's all the budgeting I ever got. I'm not blaming my money management issues or the lack there of on anyone else that was my responsibility to learn.

I really didn't start being financially responsible until the late 90's.

My youngest son, De'Vante, had to be about 3 and I was having the hardest time. I was working 12 hours a day 7 days a week, trying to pay my bills, still parting on the weekends, and trying to raise four children by myself. I was living in my cousin's house on Dever Street in Rockmart. I want to tell you this story because it was a very eye opening experience in my life and it was when I learned that I had to do better the money God gives me because he was not going to keep giving it to me.

During this time in my life I started to become more spiritual or shall I say as I started to reconnect with my spiritually and all hell started breaking loose in my life.

My cousin and her husband had been working with me to purchase a house that they owned. Through several months of late payments and other things they just could not continue to allow me to live there. They had a family of their own that they were providing for. I am sure that my lack of financial responsibility also put a strain on theirs. They were kind, they were patient and they were real. After they had done all they could do to help me, they had to decide to sell the home. They had to come and tell me that I was going to have to move. I will never forget how hurt I was. I felt like I had disappointed them, my kids and MY SELF. I wanted to just ball up and die. I sat there in my chair and just cried and told my aunt to go get my Mama. When Mama came to the house, with tears in my eyes I told her what happened. We sat in the house, I cried my eyes out and I told her I'm just tired of struggling. This time I wasn't playing on her "Mom emotions" because I didn't need any money. I was honestly tired. All Mama could do was be real with me. She told me something that I remember until this day and I believe it's what really kept me from having a mental break. She said, "I know you are tired and all I can tell you is this, hang on in there I know it's hard but it seems like when they all get in school things will get a little better." That might not seem like much to you but for some reason that day all I needed was my Mama to give me some type of hope and she did. I held on to those words and I kelp pushing. I ended up moving back home with my four children and about a year later I bought my first house.

Not being a good manager of my money has cost me a lot over the years and I don't just mean material things. It's embarrassing to have your utilities cut off or your belonging being set on the streets, being turned down for loans or not having your own place to lay your head.

I'm not going to tell you that I have it 100% down packed. I still mess up but no where near how I used to be. There were some hard lessons that I had to learn along the way. It's my sincere prayer that this message helps you to recognize if you have some of the same patterns and help you to forgive yourself and move forward.

Internal Release: *Breathe in and out 5 times slowly and repeat aloud in the mirror: I am a good steward/guardian over the finances that are entrusted in me. I have more than enough to get what I need and what I want.*

Declaration of Spiritual Restoral: *Lord thank you for helping me do the right thing with my money. I will learn to budget and plan my resources to meet the needs of your household and my household. The Bible declares that you will supply all of my needs according to your riches in Glory. Lord in you there is no lack and I will stand on your word. In Jesus name.*

BUDGET TIPS

1. **Make it a point to be thankful for planning your budget!**
2. **Write your financial obligations in a notebook and review them in the same intervals as your pay schedule.**
3. **Don't compare your money to anyone else's**
4. **Write a "my treat" plan into your budget (up to 5%) of your monthly net income (bring home).**
5. **Plan your rainy-day fund**
6. **Decide on your charitable contributions and include that in your budget.**
7. **Split your payments up when ever possible.**
    a. **Example. If you get paid each Friday and your mortgage/rent is $600, then take $150 a week out of your check and put it to the side for rent. For the months that have 5 weeks put that extra in your rainy-day fund.**

If you have the workbook; at this time, please complete the exercises for today.

Day Six: I forgive me for not being a cheerful giver

Day Six: I forgive me for not being a cheerful giver. Man, oh mannn I think this one may be my most favorite one yet! People who know me know that I am a giver. I will give a person just about anything I have. Except for my food HAHAHAHAHA. My family teases me about this because I will seriously give a person anything but my food. Now I will buy you something, but I will not be giving you mine. With all jokes aside, I want to talk a little about not being a cheerful giver.

I started in the ministry when I was thirty-three years old. When I started preaching, I wanted to do everything right. I thought to myself, I can let people see me do this, I can't let people see me do that. I got to give, I got to help those in need, I got to ***"pay"*** *my tithes, I got to do this I got to do that. I mean I had so many can'ts and ain'ts attached to my spirit I almost ran myself crazy trying to portray an image that I thought people should see instead of going to my natural progression the way created me to be. I remember all the pressure I put on myself to make sure I* ***paid*** *my tithes because I felt like God was going to punish me if I didn't. If the church asked for any type of assessment for one of our programs, you* *best to believe I had mine right there in my hand being certain that people saw me drop it in the plate so they would know I did MY part. All the while I was not feeling the manifestation of joy and abundance that I thought giving money would give me. There would be times that I would* ***pay*** *my tithes and by the end of the week I wouldn't have a cent to my name and would be sitting there disappointed in God because I was not getting blessed like I thought he was going to bless me or shall I say how I thought he* ***should*** *bless me. I had the mind set and the scriptures to go with it. I was trying to hold God accountable for his word because I was following the* *instructions of the word but not the spirit of the word.*

I know you may be wondering what the spirit of the word is versus the instruction of the word is. I will give you an example Malachi 3:10 (NIV)states Bring the whole tithe to the storehouse so that there will be food in my house. Test me in this, "says the Lord Almighty," and see if I will not throw open the floodgates of heaven and pour out so much blessing that there will not be room enough to store it.

Wheewww even typing it now does something to my spirit RIGHT now! I had to stop and get me a praise break right quick!! SO, as I was saying with this scripture when I was following the *instruction of the word I did exactly what it said because I wanted to get the exact results that it said. I **paid** my tithes to the church because I expected God to bless me. To me it didn't matter that I was being mean to people, or that I was giving my last fruit instead of my first or that I was operating in fault piety. I brought the tithe, so I expected a blessing and when I didn't get one, I blamed God and not myself. I operated in the pattern with so much money and so many seeds that I called myself sowing.*

To be honest I cannot even remember the exact day when the Lord started dealing with me with this. I do remember having a conversation with my sister Courtney and she and I were talking about giving, how we were realizing that God didn't tell us to do it. I started to think about my motives in giving and I realized that my motives and my heart was not right. I thought I was doing the right thing because I was giving and blessing others but really all I was doing was satisfying my ego in the name of the Lord. I had to repent, and I remember saying to myself Lynne you did not know any better but now that you know you must do better. There were so may people that I helped that I should not have and so many people that I should have helped but I couldn't because I have given their blessing to someone else because I was ego tripping. I am by no means telling you not to give to the church or not to bless others but what I am telling you it to check your motives.

When you operate in the spirit of giving you ***bring*** *your tithes you don't* ***pay*** *it, you don't put it last and you surely don't miss it at the end of the week.*

Internal Release: *Breathe in and out 5 times slowly and repeat aloud in the mirror: I am financially blessed and it is my joy, my honor and my pleasure to not only bless the house of the Lord with my first fruits but it is my joy, my honor and my pleasure to bless whoever whenever HE tells me to!!*

Declaration of Spiritual Restoral

Lord thank you for teaching me to give in good pleasure. Whether it be my money, my talents, my possessions or my time; help me to do it all to your glory. Thank you for teaching me how to give in the spirit of your word. In Jesus name Amen

Give and it will come back to you
good measure pressed down
shaken together and running over
will men give unto your bosom

If you have the workbook; at this time, please complete the exercises for today.

Day Seven: I forgive me for not enjoying my youth

Day Seven: I forgive me for not enjoying my youth. Awe man, whenever people write books like these, I'm sure it gets awkward when it is time to tell about their childhood. Well I guess I can say for me it is awkward because for me I am laying it all bare. The memories I have are my memories and my perceptions so they are neither right nor wrong they "just are"? It wasn't until I became a "Self proclaimed awaken adult" did I realize my Mama and Daddy was going through their issues of life while raising eight children just like I did while raising four. Just like it was not easy for me I'm sure it wasn't easy for them.

As I became an adult, I realized I had the best parents in the world. They were not perfect but when I became a paren,t I realized I was not a perfect one either.

Sidebar: I had to come over here to talk about "being woke". There are so many stages to this thing called life. We never really have all the answers. It seems like every time we think we are there…we have an awakening or an epiphany if you will. When I started having these it was in my early 20's I think that was when I started looking for a greater meaning to life. I started finding my way and my spirit started showing me things that I didn't see. So, my friend you are going to "wake up" so many times before you leave here. Just embrace the alarm clocks in your spirit and use the knowledge to become a better version of yourself.

It's hard for me to decide how long I want this chapter to be because there is so much to share.

I remember having a good childhood. It was like we always had fun. To me my Mama and Daddy were like superheroes. They were good providers and we never wanted for anything. They taught us to treat people with respect and to respect ourselves. We weren't the kind of family that said I love you as we were growing up. I think my parents thought we knew they loved us.

I mean what parent doesn't love their child right? Now, as an adult, I know that my parents loved me but that was something that I didn't know as a child or feel as a child. To me, despite having a roof over my head, clothes on my back food on the table etc. etc., I didn't feel like my parents loved me because they didn't tell me, and they didn't hug on me. When the fact was there was eight of us and our parents loved us so much, that my Daddy worked all kinds of hours in an environment that was not always favorable to black people; that's love.

My Mama took a job in the cafeteria and worked the same hours as our school hours so that she could be home to take care of us in the evenings. That's love.

Nevertheless, not feeling that and not hearing that as a child affected me in a negative way and I made selfish (childish) decisions that had adult consequences. Those negative consequences altered my life in a way that caused so may negative things to happen to me and that I internalized for most of my adult life.

I want to be clear and I want to make sure if you are a teen, young adult, in your 30s or even up through your older years and you a reading this book, take some time to do some self-reflection. In some cases, it was not your parents' fault for bad decisions that you made and even if it was, I am giving you permission to take that power back by forgiving them and forgiving yourself.

Coming up Daddy didn't go to church but him and Mama made sure we went. Every time I spent the night with either one of my grandmothers it was a guaranteed thing that was going to Sunday school and Church. I loved going to church and I was into it too. I remember when I was about thirteen years old, I was staying on the hill in my parents' yard and I was talking to the Lord and I said Lord, I know I am young but tell me what you want me to do? He said I want you to do that. I said: "Do what"? he said "That". I looked to the right. I have to pause right here and set the stage. From my parent's house if you are facing the street and look to the right there is a cross (on a church) that is visible from about a quarter of a mile away. So, when I asked God what he wanted me to do and he said that. I said "What preach" and he said "yes". I said

"Lord I'm only a child I haven't even got to experience life yet". He asked, "Do you want to experience life?" I said "Yes", he said "Ok" and that was all he said. He never bothered me about preaching again until I was about twenty-seven years old.

So, from that day I started "living life". It really wasn't living life it was really digging a whole for myself that got so deep I almost didn't make it back.

It seemed like once I told God I wanted to experience life I started getting bombarded with so many different things good and bad. The more I tried to hold on to my good nature the more the bad nature showed me how much I was missing.

See when I was coming up, I never thought I was cute. I was scrawny, my teeth were crooked, and my ponytails were always going every which way but the right way. I would always look at my four BEAUTIFUL sisters and wonder why I didn't look like them. I had very low self-esteem. Then add on top of that I had a high need for attention that wasn't being met because I had to share the limelight with seven other siblings. It was a recipe for disaster once puberty hit.

2nd Grade

3rd Grade

4th Grade

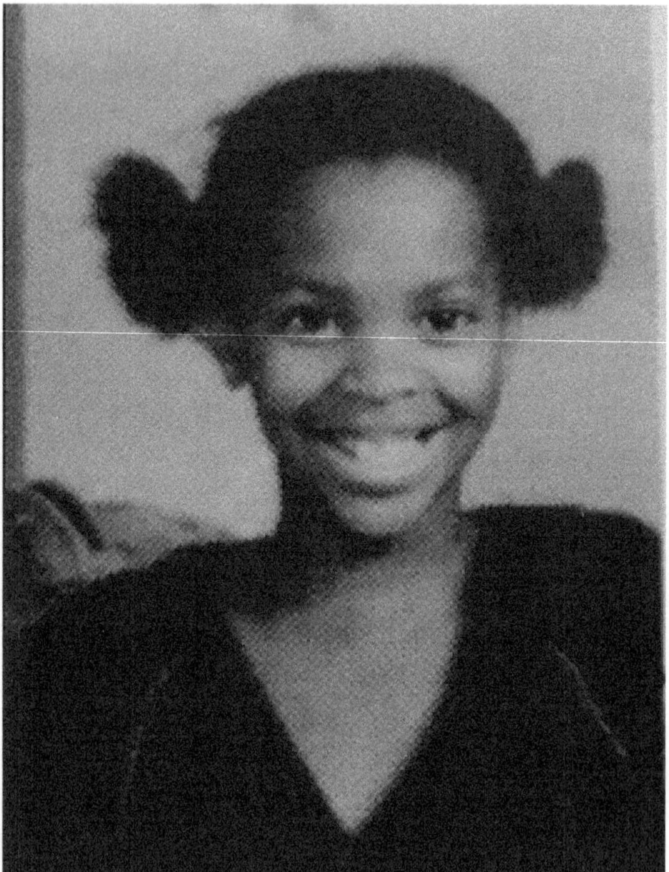

5th Grade

When I hit puberty, I started to fill out. I got boobs and butt. I was very curvy, and I liked the attention that the new body got for me. It wasn't good attention, but it was attention none the less.

I mentioned earlier that my parents were doing what they knew to do to raise and provide for eight children while they were going through their issues of life and part of those issues of life involved some infidelities involving my Dad. I let my Mama read this before you guys so that she won't be caught unaware. I told y'all a lot of things changes for me when I was about thirteen. I used to hang out in the projects in our neighborhood and there was a group of friends that I hung with now this entire family had apartments in the housing projects. The Mama lived in one project and all the daughters had a project in the same area. My friend and I spent a lot of time running from all the auntie's houses. I used to always see my Dad at one of the Aunties' houses, but I never thought anything about it until one day we were at the Auntie's house and my Dad came over there. He was very nonchalant about being there and did not act shocked at all that I was there. It was like something clicked in my brain and I realized my Daddy was cheating on my Mama with my friend's Aunt. MY WORLD CRASHED. There was an anger and a hurt that consumed my spirit and I change. My little mind, my little thought processes, my feelings toward men, my feelings toward my Daddy my feelings toward my Mama it all change. I started rebelling against everything that my Dad and life represented. I remember thinking "I cannot tell my Mama this because I don't want to be the one responsible for breaking up our family. Can you imagine being thirteen with that kind of burden in your spirit? Well I was. I thought I got to do stuff to make Daddy stay home. I started acting out and getting in trouble in school. I figured if I stayed in trouble so much then Daddy would have to be home seeing why I was acting up he would have time to go see Theresa. That didn't work though he didn't stop, and I didn't stop. To be honest with you I don't even think he noticed. It was like everything he asked me to do I did the opposite. I was a hurt little girl taking on grown up problems.

I begin to drink, and smoke weed at thirteen years old and my parents never knew. Me and one of my cousins passed weed in school, we had grown men buying us liquor and beer and we were promiscuous. Yep at thirteen.

My teen years weren't my best years. I won't sit here and blame anyone or anything on the years not being so good. It was almost like I was living a double life. I was so sneaky with my mess, I was maintaining good grades in school and even participating in the band, but under cover I was an evil little force to be reckoned with.

If you are a young adult reading this book and you have had a traumatic experience dealing with something that you feel like you can't tell anyone or that the impact of telling your truth is going to be bad for everyone else I urge you right now not to hold that in. If you held things in your spirit in the past, I urge you, as a matter of fact I GIVE YOU PERMISSION to let it go. For a long time, I tried to make my Daddy a villain or even look at my Mama's good heart as being weak simply because he made a mistake and I let that anger and hurt take control of me. You don't have to do that.

Side bar: Weak woman. My Mama didn't act a fool like I thought she should have. She didn't bust the windows out of Daddy's car she didn't fight the woman. She sacrificed and stayed an extraordinary woman of class, a wife and she raised her children. My mind couldn't comprehend her actions as being strong then but I do now. See we were the prize and she made sure that we were provided for despite the situation she was in. That's a strong woman

Internal Release: *Breathe in and out 5 times slowly and repeat aloud in the mirror: I am thankful for the life I have lived I am victorious over the disappointments of my childhood.*

Declaration of Spiritual Restoral:

Lord thank you for delivering me from myself. SO many years I blamed myself for things that I could not control. Thank you for the freedom you have given me today. In Jesus name amen.

Traumatic release

Sometimes visiting the past brings up old hurtful feelings that a book alone cannot help you overcome. Some people tend to bury the experiences so deep down inside that has negative emotionally crippling effects on their entire life. Please don't be ashamed to seek professional help from a license Therapist.

If you have the workbook; at this time, please complete the exercises for today.

Day Eight: I forgive me for not being a good mother

Day Eight: I forgive me for not being a good mother. If you ask a little girl what she wants to be when grows up, most of the time she says I'm going grow up, get married and have x amount of kid. I was just like that I had it all planned out in my mind. Going to grow up, go to college to become a criminal defense lawyer, get married and have four children (My oldest son just turned thirty. Every t boys & two girls). The truth of that story is I got pregnant at seventeen and I thought that dream was over for me.

I've already told y'all that I was very promiscuous as a teen because I was looking for love and attention in all the wrong places. I had put myself in situations where I was messing with and flirting with adult men, some married and some not; I didn't care, I didn't have any remorse about and I wasn't scared. I had made up in my mind that no men were any good and that I was going to get them before they got me. That worked for me for years, until I got caught off guard.

It was like something out of the movies. My cousin's Dad had passed away and we were all around for the funeral. This fine dark chocolate man with the prettiest smile I had ever seen came to my Aunts house to see my cousin who was his half-brother (for the sake of his privacy we will call him William). I instantly zeroed in on him and staked a quick claim. He had a nice car, he was on leave from the Navy and looked like a million bucks. I was instantly drawn in. I was sixteen (about to be seventeen) and he was twenty-six. I didn't care I was in full rebellion mode and was going to do what I wanted to anyway. My Daddy didn't allow boys to come see us so we all used to meet them on the road on the side of the house and sneak off anyway, so this wasn't any different. He took me places to eat, he bought me little stuff, he talks about us having a future together when I graduated high school, I mean he treated me like no one ever had and as far as I could tell we were in love.

This went on for a while and I ended up getting pregnant in 1988. I hid it from my parents until I was about six months along. I wasn't going to tell it then, but my Mom worked in the high school cafeteria and one of my friends asked her when my baby was due and she say she didn't even know I was having a baby!! Man, what a way to find out. Anyhow I bet you can imagine how that conversation was after school. After I told my parents I ended up spending a lot of time with William and his Mama. She was always nice to me and encouraged me to finish school.

There is an old saying that "when things seem too good to be true; they usually are", well that's the story of my life.

When I was about seven months pregnant William and I were at his Mom's house and there was a knock on the door. His Mom' room as in the front of the house so she had answered the door. She came and knocked on the door and told him to come here for a minute somebody was at the door. It didn't seem strange to me so I didn't bother with it, but soon I could hear some yelling coming from the other room. So, I went in there. When I got in the room there stood a lady looking angry and broken hearted. Her and William were arguing about him cheating on her with me! Mind you I already told y'all I had been running men sense I was thirteen, so I wasn't fazed by her standing there looking at me crazy as a matter of fact I looked at her just as crazy as she was looking at me. The confrontation was not what shocked me it was what she said to me that was the worst gut punch I had ever had up to that point.

The first thing she said to him was that he should be ashamed because I was only a baby and that he had ruined my life. She didn't directly get smart with me but when I told her don't worry about me being a baby, she just looked me in the eyes and said "He been lying to you just like he lied to me. That's my car outside and I'm taking it when I leave. He ain't got no money and I hope you know if on crack!" When she said that I was like time stopped I looked at his Mama like she was going to say "No he isn't" but she didn't say a mumbling word and it was like something in my spirit clicked and I went from loving him to hating him and all the grand dreams I had crashed right in my face. Something in me said you got to get it Lynne and I went into survival mode and this what I did for the last thirty years.

I had two more failed relationships and three more children. In each situation I found myself carrying the burden to providing for children by myself that I create by myself. I love my children with all my heart, but my heart was so hurt, so weary, so burden down, so broken, so hard, and so disappointed (in myself) that I didn't enjoy being a mother. I did it because I was obligated to do it. My children didn't ask to be here, so it was my job to provide for them and raise them a make sure they did not go without. I treated raising my children like it was a duty and not my pleasure. I wasn't always soft or affectionate towards them and I should have been. I was very ridged. It was like I was always playing defense because I saw how the world had treated me and I be damned if I let it chew them up and spit the out. My intentions were good, but the process was wrong. I can say I was not always the best mother. Yes, I dressed them nice, I gave them a lot of things when my money started getting right, but I also exposed them to some things and some people that I shouldn't have. Now that they are adults, I look back over it and I realize I should have let them see and feel the softer side of my personality. I should have sacrificed in a different way. Being a parent is hard. Children don't come with an instruction book, but one thing you must do is get the balance. I regretted so many things that I didn't do, and I felt guilty for so long. I had to forgive myself for it and stop trying to make up for things that I did not do for them when they were children but to now help them to become better adults.

Maybe you have been in this situation or are in it right now. Maybe you have grown adult children and you see things that they are doing, and you wonder what you could have done differently or maybe you are holding some type of guilt because of how things turned out for them. Forgive yourself for it!

Internal Release: *Breathe in and out 5 times slowly and repeat aloud in the mirror: I am a good Mother/Father. I have provided for my children and shown them love. I have replaced any lack in our relationship with more attention to the details of their lives. I love my children and they love me.*

Declaration of Spiritual Restoral:

Lord I thank you that I have a chance to be a better Mother to my children than I have ever been. Lord thank you for helping me to heal and see my faults. I cannot turn back the hands of time, but I can move forward from where I am now! I love you Lord and I thank you. In Jesus name AMEN!

Man, oh MAN I loved that chapter!!

Mini Exercise

Whether it's a single parent situation, co-parenting situation or even a marriage with your own children or blended family, take some time to do emotional inventory. It doesn't matter if the children or adults or not, it is never to late to mend relationships or improve on them. Below are five points to get you started. Remember this is not professional advice. If you feel you need a third party to facilitate your session with your child/children, DO NOT be ashamed to seek professional help!

1. **Forgive yourself**
2. **Set up time to speak with your child**
3. **Don't defend their perception**
    a. **For example, if they say something you don't like don't say "That's not true" because to them it's their truth**
4. **Sincerely apologize.**
5. **Work on a plan that you both agree on to mend the relationship. Take small steps!!**

If you have the workbook; at this time, please complete the exercises for today.

Day Nine: I forgive me for pretending to be someone else just to fit in.

Day Nine: I forgive me for pretending to be someone else just to fit in. I'm going to let this one marinates for a minute. It's late on a Sunday evening and I'm trying to pick a place to start. Tears are welling up in my eyes because I am thinking about how I felt as a kid when I experienced these things. Even as I write and think of the people who did this to me, I wonder if they even realize they did it. I wonder if they realize the hurt that it caused me. For a long time, I felt some type of way about these people. I forgave them but as I sit here in the process of forgiving me, my heart hurts a little. Remember in a previous chapter I shared with you all that my self-esteem was low. I spent a lot of time thinking about how ugly I was how ugly my clothes were and how ugly my hair was. I lived this every day. I can't say that it was true but it's what I thought about myself.

I had (and still have) a cousin who everyone would always say was so pretty. We will call her Egypt; she was popular and had a lot of friends. She and I were inseparable coming up and did a lot of things together. For a long time she and my other cousins were the only friends that I had and I would have been fine with our lives staying like that, but as I said she was popular, and ***<u>she</u>*** *had a lot of other friends that we hung around with.*

Side bar: Hey check in on your children. They are bombarded with so much other stuff that we weren't. If they are feeling anything like I was from elementary through around the 10th grade, then they need someone to talk to. Even if you have another friend or relative that they trust who can check with them. My negative self-speak developed very early and it shaped my mind set for a lot of bad decisions I made as a teen and adult. Intervene early and often.

I always felt like the odd person out because I did not dress or look like they did. I often felt like they were talking about me when I wasn't around. I made every effort to fit in. I wasn't a comedian, but I started do things to make everyone laugh so I could feel like there were laughing with me instead of laughing at me. I remember I used to fake having a laughing spell just so everyone could laugh too. When I really wanted to cry.

In every group you have the Alpha then everyone else takes their spot after that. In our group, Egypt was clearly the Alpha. She had a power over out group that I don't even think she realized she had.

When we were in middle school, our group would meet every morning and chill in the gym until it was time for class. This particular morning was a little different than normal. See Egypt and I had a disagreement the day before and we were not speaking. Mind you I did not have an argument with anyone else in the group, yet when I got to the gym and proceeded to sit down with them, NOONE spoke to me at all. I mean they acted like I did not exist. I was completely devastated. I got up got and left. I felt embarrassed, humiliated and alienated. I went on to class and pouted the entire day. We all walked to school so even at the end of the day I walked home by myself. The thing about the arguments between Egypt and I is that they never even lasted a full day so by the time we both got home and got our homework done we were calling each other and right back best friends. Guess what they next day her friends were speaking to me like nothing ever happened.

This same thing happened to me a few times and what I learned most out of each situation is I had to have my own friends, never do anyone how they had done me and to be a leader not a follower. I made a point not to be like that towards anyone because I remembered how it made me feel when it was done to me.

Internal Release: *Breathe in and out 5 times slowly and repeat aloud in the mirror: I am glad to be my authentic self. ALL of my imperfections are perfect. I am genuine, kind, loving and honest. I treat people with honor and respect no matter who you are!!*

Declaration of Spiritual Restoral:

Lord thank you for helping me to realize that I was always beautiful inside and out. Thank you that through this bad experience as a child I learned to be a humble, trustworthy, honest and loyal friend. Thank you that you thwarted another trick that they enemy devised to destroy me! I love you and I thank you so much. In Jesus name.

If you have the workbook; at this time, please complete the exercises for today.

Day Ten: I forgive me for not always being a good wife.

Day Ten: I forgive me for not always being a good wife. This is a heavy hitter. If you ask most women, they will talk about how good of a wife they are. How they cook, clean, meet all their husband's needs blah blah blah. It may be true. I can say that I do some of those same things, but I also can say there is a lot of things that I did not do.

My husband and I have been married going on ten years now. Our courtship and marriage was not the ideal situation. I knew him from around the neighborhood and we officially met through a family friend. In the beginning

I was apprehensive to talk to him but later he and I started talking on the phone and spending a little time together. There were things going on in both of our lives and I wanted a real relationship that he was not able to give me. Near the end of 2007 he ended up getting arrested and was incarcerated

About a year later we reached out to me and things progressed from there. I never took myself to be a person who would talk to someone in jail. I never had done anything like that, but I had a love and attraction for Randy that I just could not shake.

We were married at Telfair State Prison in Helena GA on January 29, 2010. No one was there but him, my Pastor and me. Our wedding was witnessed by one of the guards at the prison. I was ok with that because I loved him, and I knew it was the right decision for me.

It was a long eight years and it was difficult on both of us. We had some major setbacks in our relationship due to somethings that both of us did what damaged our trust. In a moment of anger and uncertainty I started to question if getting married to a person in jail was the best decision. I constantly found myself thinking "Why be faithful to him, ain't no telling who he is talking to now and or what he gone do when he gets home. All you are doing is making a fool of yourself". Before I knew it, I started to resent my husband. Every day I dwelled on past issues that we had. I was mean to him when he called and had stopped emailing him. It seemed like the very moment I was dealing with keeping my faith strong and being faithful a man just showed up out of the blue.

Sidebar: I must share some information with you all so that you can put things into context. I started preaching when I was 33 years old. I started spending time with Randy when I was 36. We got married when I was 38. I spent a lot of time praying and asking God to save and change him, but really it was me that still needed some deliverance.

This man was someone that I knew since we were very young. I knew it was wrong to even have the conversation with him, but I convinced myself that it was innocent. I mean what could go wrong. I was saved, I was married, and I had not intention for cheating on my husband. That's not what happen though. One conversation led to another and me and this person ended up having sex. I was wrong I was dead wrong. The cost for making that mistake has been really devastating to my marriage. We've gone through a rough patch for so long I had begun to think that every time something bad happened between us it was God paying me back for cheating. God is not like that. It was really punishing myself and allowing my husband to punish me. I forgive me for being unfaithful. I forgive me for being hard hearted towards my husband and I forgive me for leading another man astray when I knew better.

Being married is nothing to play with and being married to someone that is incarcerated is entirely different experience within itself. I have had countless people contact me asking about my experience and I tell them all the same thing. A person must be sur that being married to someone in jail is what they are able to do. There is a different mental and spiritual devotion that a person needs to be able to weather that type of storm. Not only does your faith in God have to be strong, but your fidelity must be strong, your communication has to be honest and your mind had to be able to endure the loneliness and separation. Sometimes people think they can do it, but it's not has easy as people think.

Internal Release: *Breathe in and out 5 times slowly and repeat aloud in the mirror: I am an excellent wife. I am honest in my communication with my husband and shows him the attention and affection and affection that he deserves.*

Declaration of Spiritual Restoral:

Lord thank you for still loving me despite me. I am so thankful that my mistakes do not define me. Thank you for showing me a part of my flesh that was not dead and thank you for delivering me from myself. I thank you for continuing to heal and restore my marriage. In Jesus name AMEN.

If you have the workbook; at this time, please complete the exercises for today.

Day Eleven: I forgive me for not cultivating my relationship with God

Day Eleven: I forgive me for not cultivating my relationship with God. My relationship with God is the most important relationship that I will ever have, and I have neglected for the better part of 20 years.

I have the ability to break down a scripture into context that a little child can understand. I can expound on a subject with references and current day analogies so that relates to both my young and my old audiences. However, even with being able to do all of that. I didn't have an intimate relationship with my creator. Even in all of this he kelp me covered when he could have exposed me and been right in doing so. I used to talk to God all of the time, but I never listened to God not one time. I treated him like an ATM or something. I would put my prayer in like my debit card and receive the blessing like cash coming out of the dispenser. I don't hardly recall ever listening for responses from him because I didn't need one. My thought was: I tell him what I want, he does it, and "boom" we are done. It would send me in to an emotional wreck when ever God did not "dispense" the "blessing" when and how I wanted him to. There were so many times that I was so disappointed in God because he did not do what I wanted him to do when I wanted him to do it. I completed discounted what I was teaching. OH, WHAT A HYPOCRIT I WAS.

Matthew 6:33 (NIV)

But seek first His kingdom and His righteousness, and all these things will be given to you as well.

All we have to do is look for HIM first and He will take care of everything we need, want and desire~

Do you see yourself in some of the things I am saying? I forgive me for neglecting you Lord because my negligence has costed me so many years of experiencing your divine direction for my life. I would often find myself listening to my Pastor speak and would be thinking to myself "Boy he really told them" when he was talking to me too.

God has been so good not to strike me dead or expose my mess while I was in the mess. He had covered and protected me beyond anything I could ever think of. I had a nerve to wake up daily and be mad at him because I did not get a certain job or have x number of clients for my business.

Internal Release: *Breathe in and out 5 times slowly and repeat aloud in the mirror: Lord you and I have the best relationship on Earth. You talk to me and I listen. You clothed me with love and kindness and your tender mercies!! Thank you so much.*

Declaration of Spiritual Restoral

Lord thank you for teaching me how to spend time with you. Thank for teaching me how to listen to your responses. Thank you for teaching that my prayers should not only be asking you for stuff. Thank you for teaching me to worship and love your presence. In Jesus name, Amen.

Cultivate your relationship with God.

1. ***Spend a set time with God. Just you and him***
2. ***Pray to hear his voice and then listen for your prayer to be answered.***
3. ***Worship him in spirit and in truth. NO need to fake it with God***

If you have the workbook; at this time, please complete the exercises for today.

Day Twelve: I forgive me for thinking it was my fault that I was molested.

Day Twelve: I forgive me for thinking it was my fault that I was molested. Molestation comes in so many forms, sometimes verbal, a slick touch, dry humping or the worst – penetration. It never matters what form it is, it's all bad when the victim cannot consent or does not consent to what you are doing. Just sitting here trying thinking over my life I have remembered at least twenty times I was either fondled, inappropriately kissed, inappropriately touched, pulled in a corner, taken off in a car, taken in a the woods, and even held down on the bed by people that I was in a relationship with. None of the memories are welcomed memories. I always blamed myself for being too fast/provocative (better known by society as "asking for it"), too weak to fight them off or too dumb to know what they were doing. This had happened to me so many times as I was coming up, I started to think it was a normal way of life. I really started using it to my advantage to get weed, liquor and beer "for free". I really could write a separate book on all the things and all the people who performed a sexual act with me or to me. As I became an adult and started replaying some of the things that happen to me, I started to blame myself. I even wondered sometimes why I didn't tell anyone. I guess it was the nature of my mind. Some of these men (AND WOMEN) had families then and how and me telling on them would ruin that. Most of the time I had my behind somewhere I wasn't supposed to be so in my mind I was thinking about how bad I would get in trouble not about how wrong they were for molesting me. I was exposed to sexual acts way before thirteen, but I did not experience full penetration until I was thirteen.

I don't really remember how old I was, but I remember what happen. I was always somewhere playing with other children and this particular day was not any different. Me and a group of children were playing with some older children and one of the girls asked if I wanted to playhouse. We all said yes and so she began to assign the Mama and Daddy and we proceeded to play the game. Sometimes it would be all girls and sometimes it would be some boys with us. This girl would always have us pulling down our clothes and hunching with each other. Sometimes the boys would hunch on us and sometimes she would have the girls hunching on each other. I wasn't until I got older that I realized what we were doing. For many years I struggled with my sexual identity and experienced sexual deviance as result of being exposed to sexual role play at such an early age. I used to blame myself for not telling and I often wonder how many other children that this happen to. I could have been a voice, but I didn't do or say anything to anyone until today.

Another time was when I was about fourteen, I used to go visit some people who were very close to my family. I have changed this story a little because if I say certain things people who know me and know them will know who I am talking about and at this point they are no longer together and I love her too much to hurt her in this way. As I was saying I had some people that I visited a lot and this particular day the wife had left me at home with her husband. I was in the room sleep and he came in the room and touched my butt. I jumped up scared to death because I knew what was about to happen and he said "Come on don't be acting scared I know you giving them boys some from Rockmart you gone give me some too with them little shorts on" I was terrified. I screamed and cried and begged and he was just groping all over me. The only thing that saved me that day was my period was on so he couldn't mess with me. When the wife got back home, I DID NOT SAY A MUMBLING WORD I just told her I wanted to go home. He sat in his chair with a beer in his hand looking at me like you better not tell shit.... guess what I didn't. I went home and I never went to their house again. The whole time I kept blaming myself because I ***was*** *having sex and instead of me focusing on the fact that* *this creep had just tried to rape me, I was thinking about who could have told him and that it was my fault because I should not have had on short shorts around him. This is just two of the many situations that I found myself in. This kind of stuff happened to me so much I started to use it as my benefit and to get stuff from men. I didn't have any respect for me, I didn't have any respect for them and if they were married, I did not have any respect for the wife or girlfriend either. I always thought it was my fault because of the way that I presented myself. Not one time did I blame these perverts for preying on me. I had to say it to myself and I will tell you. If you have been in any type of sexual assault IT IS NOT YOUR FAULT and don't ever blame yourself for it. Don't ever let what someone had done to you change your view of who you are. You are fearfully and wonderfully made. You are beautiful inside and out.*

Internal Release: *Breathe in and out 5 times slowly and repeat aloud in the mirror: I am free from the grasp that sexual abuse had on me. I am no longer tied to that past and the people who did these things to me no longer have power over. I am flourishing!!!*

Declaration of Spiritual Restoral: *Lord thank you that I am finally able to speak my truth. I release the past and move forward. I am no longer bound by what others did to me. I am free*

Sexual Trauma

Some people recover from the scars of sexual trauma some people suppress them. For me journaling helps me release the anger, embarrassment and shame of all the mess that I have been through. This book is not a substitute for therapy. If you have been sexually abused, please seek help from a licensed therapy. Heal your mind, body and spirit! Remember God loves you and I love you too!!

If you have the workbook; at this time, please complete the exercises for today.

Day Thirteen: I forgive me for not respecting other people

Day Thirteen: I forgive me for not respecting other people. Once my Daddy got older and come to know the Lord, he did a lot of reflecting. Sometimes when I would talk to him and we talked about life things he would say "Lynne I have been sooo wrong in my life you would not believe." I would always say "We all have Daddy" He would say "I know" then proceed to tell me his story. I'm taking these words right out of my Dad's mouth. Y'all I have been soooo wrong in my life you would not believe it all if I told you. I thank God for his mercy and grace. I want to let you know mercy and grace does not 100% exempt you from Karma though. If you don't like to use the word Karma, I will give you some text STRAIGHT from the Bible

Galatians 6:9 KJV

"Be not deceived; God is not mocked: ***for whatsoever a man soweth, that shall he also reap"***

In other words. Make no mistake when you do not keep God's word don't think you are tricking him; whatever you are putting out in the universe is going to come right back to you. You sew love you are going to receive love; you sew deceit you are going to get deceit, you sew disrespect you are going to get disrespect.

I'm not going to say that you reap justly or by what you deserve because that does not always happen. I'm so thankful that some of my mess did not come back to me but I can tell you a lot of it has.

I told you all about me finding out about my Daddy's infidelities as a young girl. That situation had such a deep affect o me that my young brain started to build blockades up in my spirit that made me plant to dog every man out that I came across. By nature, I am soft, nurturing, loving and kind (like my Mama) but that personality wasn't working for me. I suppressed all that sweet, gentle, loving kindness and opted in to be a ridged, heartless, bitter, hateful person.

I was disrespectful to my Daddy, to my teachers, to people in my neighborhood, to other women and to the boys and men who were in my life.

My 7th grade year comes to mind as being the year that I pushed all the limits to see how bad, mean and disrespectful I could be. There was not a day that went by that I was not either drunk or high IN SCHOOL and raising hell with every teacher that I had. One that particularly comes to mind was Mr. McAdams. He was a rowdy sort and could take everything I dished out. I cannot count how many days he put me out of his class. I had another teacher that I gave the blues to as well. Mrs. Wooten. She would always tell me I was mannish just like my Daddy. When I think back on those times and how badly I treated those people I feel so bad, but today is the day I let it go. They are not around for me to ask them for forgiveness, but I hope they realized how sorry I am for how I acted.

Internal Release: *Breathe in and out 5 times slowly and repeat aloud in the mirror: Love, respect and loyalty is my portion. I am free from the guilt and shame of disrespecting others. I sew love and I reap love. I sew respect and I reap respect. I sew loyalty and I reap loyalty.*

Declaration of Spiritual Restoral: *Lord thank you that I saw the errors in my ways and changed how I treated your people. I thank you that you have not always repaid me for what I deserve. Lord I love you and I need you please continue to make me a better person daily.*

If you have the workbook; at this time, please complete the exercises for today.

Day Fourteen: I forgive me for not following my dreams

Day Fourteen: I forgive me for not following my dreams. There is a poem by the great Langston Hughes called "A Dream Deferred". It's a very short poem but it speaks volumes to how not chasing or accomplishing your dreams can make you feel.

Ever since I was a young girl, I wanted to be a lawyer. I remember in elementary school checking out the law book from the public library and just going home and reading over all the laws, sections and subsections. I had no idea what I was looking at, but I was determined that I was going to read it anyway. I don't have many regrets but if I had to chose one not getting my law degree would be it.

I've shared the story with you all about me being a teen mom and back then when people had children it was like a blessing of bring in a new life but a curse that you would have to stop all of your hopes and dreams to work in a factory to take care of your child, at least that's what I thought. For the first couple years of my oldest son's life I worked in factories trying to make ends meet so that we could have a good life. I worked in clothing manufacturing companies that mostly worked 12 hours a day 7 days a week. Around 1993 I was working at this company called Galey & Lord. It wasn't a bad job and the pay was good. As always, I worked overtime to make as much as I could to take care of me and my now two children with one on the way. I remember thinking something in my life needed to change. One day as I was working my creel I looked up and saw a gentleman who looked to be about forty maybe 50-year-old and he looked so tire, but he was pushing his buggy of yard just as hard as he could. It was like something nudged me and said "Lynne if you stay here that is going to be you in twenty years. I just couldn't do it. When I went out on maternity to leave to have my baby I didn't go back. I started going to school. I didn't get a law degree but about twelve years later I did have my bachelor's and master's degrees in Business Administration. I've done well for myself and I am thankful for the turns that my life took because I have gained a lot of wisdom and understanding along my journey.

Internal Release: *Breathe in and out 5 times slowly and repeat aloud in the mirror: Lord I am thankful to be where I am doing exactly what I am doing. I have been blessed with some great experiences in my life and I look forward to the good things I will experience next.*

Declaration of Spiritual Restoral: *Lord a dream deferred is not a dream denied. Thank you for opening doors for me I could not see and helping me to gain wisdom and knowledge to help others a long the way. I am looking forward to what is to come. Thank you for allowing me to keep dreaming~~~*

Dream Deferred but Not Denied

Tips to accomplishing your dreams at any age or economic status

1. **Write the goal 7 set small and large milestones to the finish line.**
2. **List the positives and negatives of accomplishing it (AGE DOES NOT COUNT)**
3. **Research the resources you need to accomplish the dream.**
4. **Find a mentor**
5. **Invest in yourself and the dream (time and money)**

If you have the workbook; at this time, please complete the exercises for today.

Day Fifteen: I forgive me for not lying down in the green pastures

Day Fifteen: I forgive me for not lying down in the green pastures. Lord I forgive me for not resting in your peace. Back in 1989 when that lady that my baby's Daddy was on drugs it seemed like my life got punched right out of me. It was like instantly I went into survival mode and I have been that way ever since. I am now forty-eight years of age and am just now learning how to slow down and enjoy life. I realize that in a blink of an eye I could lose everything and the world wouldn't even stop spinning one time. I've watched my parents work all their lives. Even when I started working, I believed that if I came to work and did a good job that I would always get appreciated. I learned quickly that it sometimes does not matter how well you perform or how good of a person you are, you don't always get rewarded on the job or in life. Now I make it a point to enjoy this beautiful world that I have been able to live in. I realized that I have put so much pressure on myself to succeed and be great that I have not really enjoyed the green pastures that the Lord has created for me. Does that sound familiar to you? Don't be the kind of person that works to make sure you and your family have nice things but end up so far in debt that you cannot stop working because you owe out so much. That is not enjoying life

That was me though and for the last three years I have been focusing on getting back to peace in my life and enjoying what I have already accomplished. I'm not just referring to finances, I mean in life as well.

In the 23rd Psalm verse two it states

"He makes me lie down in green pastures, he leads me beside still waters, he restores my soul"

Just think on that a few minutes. I remember when we were young, we used to play in the back yard and one of the things we liked to do is go barefoot and walk in the grass. When was the last time you just stopped and relaxed? Now is the time.

Internal Release: *Breathe in and out 5 times slowly and repeat aloud in the mirror: I am refreshed and my soul is restored.*

Declaration of Spiritual Restoral: *Lord thank you for leading me into a better place mentally, physically spiritually and financially. I am clicking the reset button in my life, in my heart and in my spirit. I am ready to enjoy this beautiful life that was created for me!! I have you to thank for it. THANK YOU, JESUS,*

Psalm 23 King James Version

The Lord is my Shepherd; I shall not want.
He maketh me to lie down in green pastures:
He leadeth me beside the still waters.
He restoreth my soul:
He leadeth me in the paths of righteousness for His name' sake.

Yea, though I walk through the valley of the shadow of death,
I will fear no evil: For thou art with me;
Thy rod and thy staff, they comfort me.
Thou preparest a table before me in the presence of mine enemies;
Thou annointest my head with oil; My cup runneth over.

Surely goodness and mercy shall follow me all the days of my life,
and I will dwell in the House of the Lord forever.

If you have the workbook; at this time, please complete the exercises for today.

Day Sixteen: I forgive me for not listening

Day Sixteen: I forgive me for not listening. If I would have listened twice as much as I talked, I know I would have avoided MANY if not all of the mess I ended up getting myself into over the years. I am not only talking about the voice of my parents, but I am also talking about the voice of the HOLY GHOST!

My parents were not the kind of parents that just sat down and talked about certain things when we were coming up. However, during my teenage years and adulthood those conversations or shall I say chastisements were there and they were accurate to life.

I recall one time I wanted to spend the night with a friend of mine and my Mama had already told me no. I decided I was going to stay anyway because that was what I wanted to do. So, I waited until it got really late and called her back and said it was too dark for me to walk home would she come and get me. She knew what my game was and she said, "No but you gone get it tomorrow". You would have thought I would have been scared but I wasn't. During the course of that stay, I saw so many people drinking and doing drugs it was unbelievable. It was an environment that I had not business being a part of. It was during this time that I became aware of so many adult men who liked to mess with teen age girls. Nothing strange happened to me that night but being exposed to that lifestyle that day was something that I never wish I would have done. The next day I didn't even go home I went to another friend's house until it got dark when I got home no one was in the living room so I called myself going to sleep on the couch so that my mom wouldn't hear me but to my surprise she waited until I dosed off to sleep and gave me a whipping that I never would forget and that I deserved. See everything that I am telling you had an impact on my life in some kind of way. That exposed to adult men who liked young girls was something that I shuck around and did all of my teenage years. I didn't have sex with all of them, but what I did was set so much bad Karma in motion over my life that it had been hard to think I deserve anything better than hard times.

My Mama didn't tell me why she said no, but years later I understand, and I wish I would have listened.

Internal Release: *Breathe in and out 5 times slowly and repeat aloud in the mirror: I listen to comprehend. Sometimes others know things that I don't, and it is best to listen so that I do not fail later.*

Declaration of Spiritual Restoral: *Lord thank you for helping me to hear when others are speaking. Thank you for helping me to not only listen but to comprehend. Thank you for releasing me from the burden that I carried when I was being defiant. I thank you for helping me. In Jesus name*

Tips for active listening

1. **Give your attention to whoever is speaking**
2. **Ask clarifying questions—This is hard when it's a parent/child relationship because the parent always want to say because I said so! I don't know if it would have help me to ask why because I had already made up in my mind what I was going to do.**
3. **Think about what you heard before you act!!!**

If you have the workbook; at this time, please complete the exercises for today.

Day Seventeen: I forgive me for not meditating.

Day Seventeen: I forgive me for not meditating. Hurry up and do this. Hurry up and do that. RUSH RUSH RUSH. If this thing doesn't make me any money by this date, then it's on to the next one. If this child doesn't come on, I'm going to leave them. If this guy does A, B or C, I am going to kick his ass to the curve. I don't have time for this I don't have time for that. Mannnn that is the story of my life. I was always in a hurry for this and that. As a matter of fact, my husband tells me that I rush into things too much. I know I do. It's like when I get my mind set on something I go in hard and then am stuck worrying about the how to accomplish it later. That is not a good place to continually put your mind and body because at some point one or both of them are going to break down.

Active meditation or meditating on purpose has become something that I look forward to. When I meditate it puts my thoughts into perspective and it helps me to get prepared for the day. I intentionally rebuke negative thoughts and focus on positive affirmations and thoughts. I use my meditation time to spend time with God and I use my meditation time to self-solve my problems. I use some of the same affirmations that I have shared in this book.

I don't want you to think that it is crazy to meditate or self-solve problems because it is not. I went through a period in my life where I did not trust anyone, and I did not have anyone to talk to about some very personal things. Mediation, positive affirmations and self-solving my problems helped me make it though. I live by it and I am thankful for it.

People will often times say, "Just pray about it" but how often do they say, "Pray about it, stay there and allow the Holy Spirit to answer"?

Internal Release: *Breathe in and out 5 times slowly and repeat aloud in the mirror: I am one with my mind, body and spirit. I will take time to enjoy every minute that I have been given. Meditation gives me perspective and balance. Thank you, Lord*

Declaration of Spiritual Restoral: *Lord thank you for helping me quiet my mind. My life was full of so many distractions that I was not focused on you or your divine will for my life. I am grounded and I hear your voice. I love you and I live in your peace. Thank you. In Jesus name.*

If you have the workbook; at this time, please complete the exercises for today.

Day Eighteen: I forgive me for careless in my actions

Day Eighteen: I forgive me for careless in my actions. Have you ever heard the saying "Hurt people hurt people"? Well I was the poster child for that saying. I was carless in my actions with how I dealt with other women. I was careless in my actions with how I dealt with my intimate relationships and I was careless in my actions in how I dealt with my children.

I decided early on that women could not be trusted, hell I was a woman that you couldn't trust. I became the character I loaded the most. I was full of hurt, anger, jealousy and bitterness. I didn't care who feelings I hurt. I should have been embracing my sisters and showing respect to them, but I didn't learn that until I was the one being disrespected. I remember once messing with a guy and he had a girlfriend, I knew he had a girlfriend and children by her, but I didn't care. It got to the point to where she called me one time. I basically told her that I wasn't going to argue with her about the guy because I didn't have the history with him that she did but that we would have the understanding that if she called him and he didn't answer he was with me and if I called him and he didn't answer I knew he was with her. When I think back on that I am ashamed that I disrespected myself and another person like that. Believe you me I paid for it later. I paid for it many years until I forgave myself. Every time I got cheated on, I thought about this person and how mean I was to her.

*I wasn't much different in my intimate relationships either. I used to have the motto that "I don't need a man for anything but **bleep**" and I made it my mission to use them for exactly that. If I saw anything flaw in them, I was on to the next one. I never gave it a second thought about how to have a good healthy relationship or how to work through problems without doing the "Tit for Tat" or turning it "rail for rail" as my Mama says. I bet you are saying in your mind "My God this girl was a* *straight up "hoe" yep I was and when I was doing it, I was proud of it. I used to brag and say, "I'm going to get them before they get me" Truth be told, regardless of how hard a woman tries to make her heart; she can never repay her heart break by breaking someone else's heart.*

Lastly, it really hurts me to acknowledge this, but I was also careless with my actions towards my children. I was always a provider, but I did not always show the affection that I should have. I didn't always take the time I should have. It is one thing to admit that to myself but a whole other thing to admit that to the world. I know I am not the only one so if me saying it will help you acknowledge and overcome your mistake in this area, then we all can heal and become a better person. It doesn't matter what their ages are if you see this in yourself mend those relationships. I'm sure my children would have much rather had me home with them than the stuff I bought, because I complained and fussed about every little thing. That was very careless of me.

Internal Release: *Breathe in and out 5 times slowly and repeat aloud in the mirror: I am attentive to the needs of those around me. I will never dishonor, disrespect or dehumanize another person. I love them just like God loves me!!*

Declaration of Spiritual Restoral: *Lord thank you for letting me see me. Thank you for helping me to love others as you have loved me. I will never be careless in my actions again. In Jesus name amen.*

If you have the workbook; at this time, please complete the exercises for today.

Day Nineteen: I forgive me for not operating in the spirit of excellence

Day Nineteen: I forgive me for not operating in the spirit of excellence. Now isn't that a gut punch? OHHHH the spirit of excellence. What exactly does that mean? I don't know what it means to you but to me it means to embody the act of being perfect in your thoughts, actions and character in everything that you do. When I think about how I haven't done this I mainly relate it to my job.

I take pride (confidence, personal ownership and enthusiasm) in my work products. I like to be timely and I like to provide deliverables as I am asked. When that does not happen I take it personal and in all of my years working I always have made appoint to ask "what are the deliverables?" and I have always done a good job at meeting deliverables and/or taking feedback to make corrections to get the deliverables.

I was working at one of the Power Plants that my company owes and had a situation at work where I was ultimately told I was not doing my job. I was abruptly sent to work at Corporate I didn't get demoted, I didn't lose my level position, but I lost my supervisor title. Anyone who knows me knows how hard I work. There were times I worked 16, 18 and 24 hours because I was learning the job, had brand new people, and had inherited a mess that needed a lot of correction. Because of how all of this went down, it was a devastating blow to me, so much so I almost did not bounce back. The only reason I stayed was because my family needed the insurance. I did the bare minimum to keep my job. I stopped being pro-active. I hated coming to work. I used to sit in my cube and cry just about every other day. I remember asking God "Lord you know I was doing the right thing in that job, I worked my behind off, why did you let these people do this to me" Y'all he never said a word. I was in a funk for about three years, then one day I was just sitting in my cube and God was like "OK Lynne, you have pouted long enough. None of that had anything to do with you. I gave some people a choice to do the right thing and they did not. They will pay for what they have done to you just like you would if you did it to someone. You have allowed their actions to get you out of character and now it is time for you to stop." SO, I DID. I learned that day that bad things happen even when you are doing your best, but sometimes it has nothing to do with you so you have to keep your head straight and keep working for God because those are His resources that you working for.

Internal Release: *Breathe in and out 5 times slowly and repeat aloud in the mirror: I OPPORATE IN THE SPIRIT OF EXCELLENCE IN ALL THAT I DO. WORK, MY FAMILY AND MY BUSINESSES ARE FOR THE GLORY OF GOD.*

Declaration of Spiritual Restoral: *Lord thank you for restoring my spirit of excellence. I almost let go but you kept me. You helped me remember why I do what I do, and it is for your Glory. Lord thank you for giving me double for my trouble in Jesus name!! Amen*

Name three things you do with the spirit of excellence.

1. ______________________________

____

____

2. ______________________________

____

____

3. ______________________________

____

____

If you have the workbook; at this time, please complete the exercises for today.

Day Twenty: I forgive me for not living my best life!

Day Twenty: I forgive me for not living my best life! There is so much around the world for me to enjoy yet I have spent most of my life making up reasons why I was not out there experiencing and enjoying life. Most of the time I would blame it on not having the money to do it, but I have been making really good money since I was about thirty-two years old so money wasn't the problem it was my managing the money that was the problem. Having money isn't the most important thing there are so many free things to do. You just have to look for them.

I would also claim that I didn't have time. Notice I said, "I claimed". Time is relative. I made time to mess with sorry men, I made time to go to the club EVERY Thursday, Friday and Saturday, but somewhere along the way when I thought about going to a museum or to the theater or to a winery, or anything new and exciting I "didn't have time". In reality I did have the time, the desire and the means, but I had just gotten so used to focusing on my defeats that I couldn't enjoy the victories that were right in my face.

For the last two years I have made it a point to go to a new place at least once a month and it has been wonderful. If you are one of those people who says "I want to do this, or I want to go there" but always make excuses not to go I CHALLENGE YOU TO STEP OUSIDE THE BOX AND DO SOMETHING DIFFENT! Even if it is just driving to a different city in your state. Find the free stuff and go do it!! YOU DESERVE IT!!

I love roses and there was a time in my life that I thought that I had to wait on a man to send them to me before I could get them. As I got older, I learned how to appreciate myself. My Mama and I planted a beautiful miniature rose bush right outside my porch and I get to enjoy them all during the year when they bloom. If you love flowers plant your own or send them to yourself! There is nothing wrong with that. As a matter of fact, I have presented you with a rose on a bookmark. Enjoy it!

Internal Release: *Breathe in and out 5 times slowly and repeat aloud in the mirror: I will make a point to do something new, go somewhere new and experience something new at least once per month. Lord you created this beautiful world for me to enjoy it and that is exactly what I am going to do.*

Declaration of Spiritual Restoral: *Lord thank you for opening my eyes to your wonderful creations in the world. I have been to some of the most beautiful places in my home state and in the United States of America. I am living my best life right now!! Thank you, Jesus!!! I cannot wait to go around the world!!*

If you have the workbook; at this time, please complete the exercises for today.

Day Twenty-One: I forgive me for not encouraging myself

Day Twenty-One: I forgive me for not encouraging myself. I was the Queen of pity party. I used to think that everything bad that happened to me because of all the bad that I had done. I would always say I deserved it. It was like I kept a check list and when a bad thing hit, I would go say "That happened because I did so and so." I was on a roller coaster of ups and downs for at least five years of my life because I was sitting back waiting on all my bad to just keeping paying me back.

When I didn't get a certain job, I would spend weeks being negative about the experience instead of creating a plan to do better the next time. If I failed on a diet I would speak negatively about my body and just say, you may as well eat it you are not going to lose weight anyway. I hardly ever had anything good to say to myself.

I couldn't see how awesome I was. I had forgotten that God does not repay everything that we do. I had forgotten that I am the head and not the tail. I had forgotten all the good things that God thought about me.

Don't forget what God has said about you either. You don't need validation from others. VALIDATE yourself! You are beautiful/handsome, intelligent, wise, and incredible!! Walk in it!!

Sidebar: Now my Daddy became the best encourager ever. As we got older Daddy changed into this person that was like a long-lost best friend. He thought that all of his children were the smartest people on Earth. He made sure everybody knew it too. He and I ended up working at the same place. He would come into my office and just sit down and talk. If we were talking about something at the Plant he would say "Listen to me now, it's the easiest thing in the world all you have to do is ___" I would just say ok Daddy I got it. I wouldn't have it but he had all the faith in the world in me and most of the time I would end up figuring it out. His approval meant everything to me!

Internal Release: *Breathe in and out 5 times slowly and repeat aloud in the mirror: I am fearfully and wonderfully made. I have the power within me to do anything that I set my mind to do!!*

Declaration of Spiritual Restoral: *Lord you are the lover of my soul. You think I am the best thing since slice bread. You said that before I was formed in my mother's womb you knew me. Lord thank you for reminding me how wonderful I am and what a wonderful life you have instore for me. In Jesus name! Amen.*

Name 5 positive things about yourself

(excluding you are a good mother/father)

1. ______________________________

____

____

2. ______________________________

____

____

3. ______________________________

____

____

4. ______________________________

____

____

5. ______________________________

____

If you have the workbook; at this time, please complete the exercises for today.

Day Twenty-Two: I forgive me for not encouraging others

Day Twenty-Two: I forgive me for not encouraging other. Sometimes people need you to encourage them in a positive way. I had got so caught up in my own mess I forgot about other people. There is an old saying "I'm taking care of me and my four and no more" well that's what I used to live by. How selfish is that? Especially coming from someone who needed help every other week.

There was a time I saw this young lady who was living a lifestyle every similar to mine. She had three children, multiple baby fathers and was raising them by herself, but like I was. By this time in my life I had started to do a little better and was going to school. I could have taken a bigger interest in her life, but I didn't. My thought was that she is going to have to learn just like I did. This young lady ended up losing her children because she just couldn't take care of them. I missed an opportunity to help her navigate through a rough time in her life. I promised myself that I wouldn't ever do that again and I didn't.

I own a small tax business in my hometown. Most of the time I end up ministering and encouraging young people about how to get a better life. I've seen so many people flourish after our conversation and I see some who come back the next year in the same situation as the last, but what I never do is bash them about it.

Internal Release: *Breathe in and out 5 times slowly and repeat aloud in the mirror: I am my brother's/sister's keeper. Every chance I get I will encourage someone to help them along the way.*

Declaration of Spiritual Restoral: *Lord thank you for giving me the heart for your people. I will encourage and speak life to them when ever you send them to me. Help me to be your mouthpiece for inspiration and encouragement. In Jesus name AMEN*

If you have the workbook; at this time, please complete the exercises for today.

Day Twenty-Three: I forgive me for gossiping

Day Twenty-Three: I forgive me for gossiping. Giiirrlll let me give you the tea. That's how we announce we have some gossip now a days. I was good at it. I talked about everybody's problems and issues regularly with no remorse or concern. I was alright with gossiping until the gossip started being about me! BOOM.

My husband and I have had a trying time since the end of 2015 and both of our cheating didn't make it any better. There was an incident in 2016 and my husband ended up being caught by the police at his side chicks house. At that time that was the most embarrassing thing that could have ever happened to me. Despite the situation, I decided to stay with him. Now mind you I am a well-known business owner, a Minister in the Church and a white-collar employee who is now the talk of the town. I turned into a hermit. I quit going to church and would have quit going to work if I could have. Every other day someone would come and tell me "what the streets was saying" and in addition to the side chick was posting on social media as if was the legit girlfriend. I was dealing with embarrassment and shame, but I couldn't didn't leave because I had cheated before he did. I took this as my get back.

The difference in what he did (this time) and what I did was that I hid mine better than he did. Everyone knew about the situation and everyone was talking about it. Through it all I held my head up and stood by my husband. Gossiping is a debilitating characteristic that is hurtful to others. We all do it because some how it makes our pitiful life look better than the other person. From that point forward I watched my mouth about being so quick to talk about another people's situation.

Internal Release: *Breathe in and out 5 times slowly and repeat aloud in the mirror: Lord, the words of my mouth speak in favor of others. I do not rejoice in someone else's downfall.*

Declaration of Spiritual Restoral: *Lord thank you for helping me to understand how hurtful my words can be. I speak goodness and healing for others in their time of trouble. Lord you are my ROCK and my REDEAMER. In Jesus name.*

If you have the workbook; at this time, please complete the exercises for today.

Day Twenty-Four: I forgive me for being a hypocrite

Day Twenty-Four: I forgive me for being hypocrite. No one is a good as they appear or want others to believe. I used to keep the appearance of being happy so that my sadness would not be so visible. I used to appear so peaceful so that my anger would not manifest outwardly. I mean after all I was saved. Aren't Christians supposed to be loving, happy, peaceful, humble, pious, kind etc. etc.? I had the look. I had the money. I knew the scriptures. I knew how to talk and when to talk. I knew how to be judgmental of others and point out their short comings and all the while I had my own character flaws that I was battling with. The sad part about it is over time I saw these same actions in other leaders of the church. We were supposed to be encouraging, leading, healing and loving on God's people, but some of us ended up wounding people worse than what they were.

For a long time, I couldn't enjoy the peace of the Lord because I had too much turmoil in my life. It was like I was living a double life. In front of people I was the person that had it together then when the doors were closed and no one could see me; all of my short comings flooded my face.

With the realization that I was hypocritical I had to start being real with myself about how I was living. I was one of those people who would mess up and use "God knows my heart" as an excuse for acting a fool. Do you know some one like that? The ones that can smile and love on everyone at church but as soon as they get home; they are hell on wheels? Well that was me multiplied timed two. Maybe that is you and you see yourself in what I have said. Well my brother/sister you don't have to keep living like.

As I started to really get close with the Lord, I decided that I didn't want to be fake anymore. I wanted peace and to really exhibit the fruit of the spirit. Lord I forgive me I forgive me I forgive me, and I give my heart to you. Create in me a

CCLLEEAANN mind, mouth, body, heart or GOD and renew the right spirit within me!

Internal Release: *Breathe in and out 5 times slowly and repeat aloud in the mirror: I am true. I am honest and I am a woman/man of good Character. I process my actions and make conscious choices to live with love, joy, peace, patience, kindness, goodness, faithfulness gentleness and self-control.*

Declaration of Spiritual Restoral: *Lord thank you for allowing me to see myself. Hypocrisy has no place in me. Lord Thank you for delivering me and restoring me. You are so good to me and I thank you for being the peace of my life! In Jesus name Amen.*

If you have the workbook; at this time, please complete the exercises for today.

Day Twenty-Five: I forgive me for worrying

Day Twenty-Five: I forgive me for worrying. There is an old saying "If you going to worry don't pray in you going to pray don't worry" Boyyy we love to say that saying while we are almost worried to death and not praying at all.

My personality is that I am a problem solver so when something happens, I go into problem solving mode and start putting out fires. Often times when people talk to me, I have to stop myself from formulating a plan to help them solve a problem. I have issues allowing things to play out.

In my younger years I suffered from insomnia because my brain could not settle down because I would be worrying about tomorrows problems every day. I took me a while to be able to pray about something and leave it God's feet. I used to be scared that he didn't hear me or if he didn't do a certain thing in X days then he was not going to do it. I finally got to the point in my life until that I had to talk myself into going to sleep. I would have to prepare for bed and do calming self-speak in order to go to sleep.

Worrying takes a toll on your body. As a result of staying up all night worrying, I would be tired, unable to focus and irritable during the day. This cycle affected my health and my relationships with others. It's only been a few years that I have learned to calm my worries and leave them in God's hands.

Philippians 4:6 NLT Don't worry about anything; instead, pray about everything. Tell God what you need and thank him for all he has done.

When I received the revelation of this scripture it changed my life.

Internal Release: *Breathe in and out 5 times slowly and repeat aloud in the mirror: MY MIND IS PEACEFUL, and I HAVE FOCUS. I am calm and the answer to my problems come at the right time.*

Declaration of Spiritual Restoral: *Lord thank you relieving me from worries. Lord I have learned to be patient and to trust you. NO good thing will you withhold from me. I thank you for helping me to result my problems calmly and logically. Thank you for keeping me in perfect peace because my mind was stayed on you!*

If you have the workbook; at this time, please complete the exercises for today.

Day Twenty-Six: I forgive me for prideful

Day Twenty-Six: I forgive me for prideful.

Proverbs 16:18 Pride goes before destruction; a haughty spirit before a fall

There is a difference between being confident and being prideful/arrogant. You really have to be careful to know which one you are operating in. I recall when I first went to work at one of the Power Plants as a Team Leader. For my company this position is a first line supervisor. Now mind you when I first started with the company, I was about a year from finishing my undergraduate degree and I was working as a union covered employee. My career path led me from being a covered employee, to an administrative representative, to a coordinator, a Comptroller (salaried position) to a Supervisor all in about five years. I worked hard for those positions and I think (well I know) I let my humbled confidence turn into prideful arrogance.

The Plant I got my first Supervisor position at was located in Carrollton GA and was a pretty good place to work at. I had my growing pains there that I attribute partly to my prideful attitude. See this plant was known to black people as one of the "prejudice plants" that was not welcoming to black people or outsiders. In my mind I was ready for "them". I expected to be treated differently and that is what I got. The people wouldn't speak to me and I would not speak to them. It got so bad that I would go in my office and shut the door. I had made up in my mind that I was going to treat them like they treated me. Y'all that was not GOOD and that was not GOD and I knew better.

I was always preparing for my next move and I had a plan in my mind of how that move was going to take place. One afternoon the Plant Manager came into my office and he asked me if I would be interested in going on shift as an Operations Team Leader. This would mean that I would have to go on shift, work nights, weekends and holidays. Now if I would have been humble and listening to what he was asking me I would have taken the position and been grateful for the opportunity. MY HAUGHTY & HIGH MINDED SELF looked that man in the face and a said "No I am not going to take that, I did not earn an MBA to work shift work" (Grasp pearls) When I look back over that conversation I wish I could have slapped my own damn self in the mouth. PRIDE GOES BEFORE DESTRUCTION AND A HAUGHTY SPIRIT BEFORE A FALL!! I messed up royally and it took me two more years to realize the gravity of turning down that offer. He was trying to put me in position to win and I spiked the ball in his face!!

It pays to pause and say let me think about it. I cannot turn back the hands of time, but I feel in my heart that my career path would have been different if I would have put my pride to the side and taken the position to strengthen my skills.

Internal Release: *Breathe in and out 5 times slowly and repeat aloud in the mirror: I am confident. I am humble. I am kind. I embody the spirit of excellence in all that I do!!*

Declaration of Spiritual Restoral: *Lord thank you for humbling my spirit. You have given me the experiences that have worked patience in me and have taught me to listen, internalize and understand before I respond. Thank you for teaching me the difference between being confident and being arrogant. I Jesus name Amen.*

If you have the workbook; at this time, please complete the exercises for today.

Day Twenty-Seven: I forgive me for being greedy

Day Twenty-Seven: I forgive me for being greedy. Yes, I mean exactly that being greedy. In fact, I mean Lord forgive me for being greedy for FOOD.

It's not going to be a long chapter but it's going to be an honest one. Eating makes me feel good. I've read the science behind it and I don't understand why I do it I just now that I do. When I have had a rough day all I want to do is come home and eat. Then the very second after I have stuffed my face, I feel bad because I know I have consumed way too much food. Even sometimes while I am eating,

I say to myself "that's enough or you are eating too much" but I still keep eating.

I've gotten better over time but the consequences of my behavior have had lasting effects on my health and my self-esteem. I have tried hypnosis, diet programs and exercise. Every time I lose a little or if I don't see results quick enough, I revert back to my old habits. This is the first time that I have even been free enough to discuss this with anyone.

To me, my food addition has the same effects on me as someone who has a substance addition.

When I eat, I have the feeling of euphoria and I just want to keep eating. My mind knows that these habits are not good for me, but I always seem to overrule my mind and do what I want to. I wake up every day feeling defeated because I can't fit a size fourteen anymore. WELL TODAY I FORGIVE ME FOR BEING GREEDY AND I TAKE MY HEALTH BACK! If this is you today, why don't you take your health back with me!!

Internal Release: *Breathe in and out 5 times slowly and repeat aloud in the mirror: I am in control of what I put in my mouth! I eat to live not live to eat. I am healthy.*

Declaration of Spiritual Restoral: *Lord thank you for helping me to openly confess my struggle. Thank you for giving me the strength and the fortitude to be delivered from the sin of greed and gluttony. Let me enjoy just enough of the right foods to sustain a healthy body weight. In Jesus name. Amen*

Weight lost tips—ALWAYS CONSULT A PHYSICIAN BEFORE STARTING ANY WEIGHT LOSS PROGRAM

1. **Journal what you are eating. How you were feeling when you were eating. What time? What portion size.**

2. **Drink a glass of water before every meal**

3. **Have a good cut off time at least 3 hours before bed**

4. **Have an accountability/exercise partner**

5. **Look in the mirror and love the body you have as it becomes the body you want!**

If you have the workbook; at this time, please complete the exercises for today.

Day Twenty-Eight: I forgive me for squandering my talents

Day Twenty-Eight: I forgive me for squandering my talents. I've already shared with you all that I always have about ten business ideas floating through my mind at any given time. I used to start a new business like every year but at the end of 2018 I realized that the ideas I was having were not always for me.

I guess I can describe it as a gift. When I get an idea in my head, I love to research it and learn the requirements for entry into what ever arena it is. My mistake in having this gift is that I try to do it all myself instead of seeking out those who have this same idea and offering my knowledge to coach them along.

My talent isn't the business idea itself; it is the ability to coach others along with their ideas. I have not been operating fulling in this because I was bogged down into thinking that I was supposed to start all of the businesses that I was dreaming about.

In the book of Exodus starting around the twenty-fifth chapter, God starts to give Moses instruction on how he wants the Arc of Covenant to be built. He is very descriptive in the materials to be used. As Moses was sitting there listening to God, I am sure he was thinking "How am I going to do all of this, this is not my skill set, but as always God comes in right on time. Around chapter thirty-one God tells Moses exactly who to get and he tells Moses "I have filled him with the Spirit of God, with wisdom, with understanding, with knowledge and with all kinds of skills"

God has gifted me with all kinds of skills, and I have spent years sitting down on those skills. I have spent thirty years of my life working for a paycheck instead of operating in my gifts. What about you? Are you operating in your gift or are you squandering your talent? Let me be clear maybe your gift is not to be an entrepreneur. Maybe its to be the best Charge Nurse, the best Teacher, the best Coach, the best housewife/husband or the best Pastor. What ever it is God has equipped you with what you need including the passion for your task.

Internal Release: *Breathe in and out 5 times slowly and repeat aloud in the mirror: I am filled the spirit of God, with wisdom, with understanding, with knowledge and with all kinds of skills. Lord I thank you!*

Declaration of Spiritual Restoral: *Lord thank you for helping me to discover what I was created to do. I love teaching people in this area. I love helping others in this area. I love learning new things. Put the right people in my path to help me expand on my gifts. Lord I thank you in Jesus name!*

If you have the workbook; at this time, please complete the exercises for today.

Day Twenty-Nine: I forgive me for doing nothing

Day Twenty-Nine: I forgive me for doing nothing. How far along would I be if I would have done "something" sooner? How many times have you said that to yourself? Time is not waiting on us. From 2012 until now. I did nothing on this book. I let it sit in my computer and in my mind. Now as I am writing I am thinking about the people that this book was meant to help. As I told y'all earlier, even though Gods timing is perfect, we can still miss the mark. I want to encourage you today. DON'T DO NOTHING DO SOMETHING!

In 2015 when I was moved out of my job I sat at my computer and I did nothing. I was stagnant and bitter and in making the choice to be stagnant and bitter I forfeited several opportunities. If you are in a situation similar to what I went through. DON'T DO NOTHING DO SOMETHING. You have to dismiss the pity party and the bitterness and muster up the ability to put bad situations behind you and move forward. You have to realize that doing nothing prolongs your ability to bounce back and recover. I spent so much time lamenting over the negative I did not have time to enjoy all the good that was going on around me.

DO SOMETHING NEW

DO SOMETHING POSITIVE

DO SOMETHING CREATIVE

DO SOMETHIG GREAT

Internal Release: *Breathe in and out 5 times slowly and repeat aloud in the mirror: I am embracing my new life. I am going to learn from my mistakes and move forward. I am recharged and ready for all the good things that are happening all around me.*

Declaration of Spiritual Restoral: *Lord thank you for waking me up. I was in a spiritual slumber and I allowed negative things to shut me down. I am doing some thing now and I vow never to allow a negative thing to distract me from your goodness. In Jesus name Amen.*

If you have the workbook; at this time, please complete the exercises for today.

Day Thirty: I forgive me for operating in the spirit of revenge

Day Thirty: I forgive me for operating in the spirit of revenge. Revenge has always been my thing. If a person did something to me; I would sit back and figure out how to do the something of equal or greater value to them. I knew it was not right, but I used to think if I did not get revenge, I was the weaker person.

I simply want you to know that seeking revenge is not worth the Karma it sets in motion. It creates a viscous cycle. A revenge artist must access the lowest fiber of his/her character to be as evil as being a revenger seeker has to get.

I have seen people let the need to get revenge ruin their entire life. I want to impress upon you today that if you have the thoughts "I'm going to get them back" don't allow those thoughts to guide your decisions. It's much better to let God take care of it for you.

Internal Release: *Breathe in and out 5 times slowly and repeat aloud in the mirror: The Lord is my avenger. He will not let me be put to shame. I stand boldly at his feet and know that he will take care of my enemies!!*

Declaration of Spiritual Restoral: *Lord thank you for calming the raging seas of my life. Thank you for helping me to trust you to be my avenger. Lord my life is in your hands. In Jesus name.*

If you have the workbook; at this time, please complete the exercises for today.

Day Thirty-One: I forgive me for allowing the past to bind me.

Day thirty-one: I forgive me for allowing the past to bind me. October 27, 2017 was the second worse day in my life. The first worst day of my life was October 19, 2015 and that was when my Daddy died. I've already shared with y'all that my marriage has been struggling for a few years and this was during the tie when it was at it worst. We had both been reeling and dealing with our own demons of things we had done in the past. I had decided to put it all behind us and focus on having a good relationship. I thought he had too, but I was mistaken.

My husband and I like to go do new things and travel and do those things. I had started writing and posting relationship affirmations and scriptures all over the house because I wanted to restore our marriage. Ii just shared with y'all that I fight the spirit of revenge badly and I was praying against my own self to be still and not do some of the same things to my husband that he had done to me. SO, the affirmations were not just for him they were for me too. I had been praying without ceasing because I was about done with the marriage. I really didn't want to start over I wanted I relationship to be better than it was before. I have to share that my husband and I have two things in common: We are both strong willed and we both hold grudges FOREVER. In this situation someone had to decide to be the bigger person and it was me. As I was saying I was praying daily and fasting once per week to get our house back right and he was doing the opposite. I recall one night during my prayer time, I was just on my knees listening and I heard the spirit of the Lord say plainly "Lynne you are about to go through some catastrophic things over the next six months but I want you to be still. Don't do anything and don't say anything" So I was like huh? No Lord you know I aint gone be able to do that. He said yes you are. And I did.

During those six months I dealt with fighting for a marriage that only one person wanted. I knew he was cheating and who he was cheating with and he started acting like since I knew it was ok. He started back messing with the same girl that he was caught with in 2016. He was being disrespectful and she was as well. Everything in me wanted to act up or go find me a man because I could. But I held on the word that the Lord had given me. "to be still" now mind you I had caught him and he together plenty of times through text messaging and snap chat messaging we would argue he would say he wasn't going to do it again and then a few days later he would be right back at it. During the month of October, I felt like things were getting better between us and I started to trust him more and started to let my guard down, but the morning of October 27, 2017 I just didn't have a good feeling in my spirit. See my husband is not a light sleeper and every morning when its time to get up (even though he was working second shift) he would still get up with me. This particular morning, he didn't get up he acted like he was so tired. I did my normal thing and got ready for work, but something told me to go down the street and then comeback, but I was running late for work so I couldn't. I went on to work but around ten that morning something told me to check my husband's email. She he had given me the password to his music app not knowing that when he saved anything to the phone it also saved it to the app. I opened the app to see a video of him and this girl having sex in our home. I instantly said GOD THIS WAS WHAT YOU WERE TALKING ABOUT!! I was devastated outside of my mind, but I wasn't shocked. Needless to say, it wasn't a good hour-long drive home but it was a good hour-long drive home because God sent my friend Cherise to minister to me and she saved my life, my husband's life and the side chick's life. I had murder on my mind.

I know you maybe thinking but what does this have to do with the past binding her? See, I've told you all story after story of the careless and immoral situations that I put myself in when I was younger. I really thought that kind of stuff was behind me but in reality, there was still somethings that had to be de dealt with. When I went through this situation God dealt with me in a way that I could only say "God you are right". I was sitting there on the steps in our house and I was thinking "Why me?" I even tried to tune up a cry and just at the very moment when I said "WWWHHHYYYY yyyoouuu lleett tthhiiss hhaappeenn?? God calmly said "Lynne uhmmm remember when you went into so and so's house three times and so and so's house two times. How could you not think this was going to come back to you." I sat there and I looked into space and I stopped crying and I didn't cry about it anymore. I was angry hell I'm still angry. That was a bitter pill to swallow and I vowed that the only thing that would stop me from getting her was if I died or if she died.

I was mad but I wasn't stupid. I just decided to sit back and wait because I was going to see her one day and it didn't matter if we were in CHURCH, I was going to get her. Y'all notice I keep saying was. God has a way of putting things into perspective for you.

I have been in the ministry since I was thirty-three years old. I love God and I love his word and one thing I won't do it taint his pulpit with my heart not right. I have not preached a word since 2017. For a long time, I accepted the fact that if I died, I knew I was going to hell because I had so much hate for him and her. It's a hard place to be in when you love and hate a person at the same time. Just recently, before the completion of this book, my oldest daughter Shay came to me and told me about a dream she had. The bottom line of the dream was that God was telling me I better let this thing go before he turns me over to a reprobate mind. My mission is too big to allow anyone to derail me. I had vacated my position for almost two years for something that these two did to me and that I had done to a few people myself. I could no longer choose to allow my anger and hurt to keep me from the plan of God. I was so bound up that I couldn't even finish the book because I wanted to be able to tell you all a good story at the end, but the truth is my husband and I are still working on this thing. Hurt goes way deep and it's hard to come back from.

There are too many people out there who need to connect with the word and work that God has set for me to do. SO, I'm saying to you maybe your situation was just like mine maybe it was worse and you allowed the bitterness, the hurt, the anger, the longing for revenge, the depression, helplessness and, the embarrassment to take over your spirit, NOT ANYMORE.

I'm not telling you to stay and I am not telling you to leave. You have to make the right decision for you. If you have had marital issues like this and you decided to stay then you have to truly forgive him/her and move forward. Lord I forgive me for letting this distraction of the past bind me and keep me away from you. I relinquish it to you today.

Internal Release: *Breathe in and out 5 times slowly and repeat aloud in the mirror: I AM FREE. MY FUTURE IS BRIGHT. I HAVE JOY AND I AM WALKING IN THE LIGHT OF THE MOST HIGH GOD.*

Declaration of Spiritual Restoral: *Lord thank you for redeeming me. I was walking in a dark place. I allowed the enemy to strip me of the mantle that you entrusted in me. I forgive me for allowing my past to follow me into my present. I stump it out at the root and I give you all Glory. The enemy meant this thing for bad but God you mean it for my GOOD. I plead the blood of Jesus over my husband and over our marriage. Your word declares that what you have put together let no man take asunder. In Jesus name!!*

If you have the workbook; at this time, please complete the exercises for today.

Marital trauma can leave a person feeling broken inside. Here are few thoughts to encourage you.

1. ***You are worthy to have the best marriage ever.***
2. ***All mistakes are not detrimental to the end.***
3. ***Seek professional therapy for support***
4. ***Pray and meditate to heal your heart***
5. ***Don't allow bitterness to take root***

Bonus Day

Bonus Day: I forgive me for

____

It's your day to put what you want to in the space. Be real and be vulnerable. Get it all out and let it all go!

Wow we made it! Whether you did this book in 31 days or 31 weeks. We are here. I know you feel better. I know there has been some sadness, some anger, some bitterness, some joy, some reflection, some journaling, some releasing, and mainly some spiritual restoration!! I laid it all bare. The good the bad and the ugly. You should too. It is time to unleash the joy of the Lord and your spirit and let your life take on a whole new meaning. It doesn't matter if you are young or old. As long as you are breathing you have the opportunity to experience the brand-new mercies that are waiting on you every morning! Today try something you have never done. As a matter of fact, take your shoes off and go walk barefoot on the grass. While you are out there don't just run out there and run back, but really let your spirit connect to the Earth. After all we were created from it. Let yourself feel all the negative energy leave your spirit and go down into the Earth. Breath in and breath out, count to ten and yell THE JOY OF THE LORD IS MY STRENGTH MY HEAVENLY FATHER HAS FORGIVEN ME AND I FORGIVE ME TOO!!

END OF BOOK

ABOUT THE AUTHOR:

Author Tabitha McClarity

A Georgia native, Mrs. McClarity has a huge impact on every individual and with every audience she encounters. She delivers a dynamic high energy message in a way that connects to and engages her audience. Tabitha has hosted and been the keynote speaker for events throughout her home state of Georgia. She encourages and educates entrepreneurs and individuals alike, helping them to better understand important aspects of being business owners from inception to implementation. Being a teen mother herself, Tabitha was able to raise four children alone and complete both her bachelor's and master's degrees in Business Administration while working full time and running a business. She comes from the school of hard knocks but decided she was not going to allow it to define her life. She is committed to assisting as many people as possible to realize their greatest potential and not allow bad life choices and decisions dictate their success. Tabitha and her husband Randy reside in Georgia where they enjoy traveling and spending time with the family.

Tabithaism – "I made some good decisions and some bad decisions, but I never let them take me out. I assess, I learn, I re-group and I come back greater!"

REFENCES

Matthew 6:14 NIV

Proverbs 6:16-19 NET

Psalm 103 KJV

Philippians 4:6 NLT

Proverbs 16:18 KJV

Galatians 6:9 KJV

Psalm 23 KJV

Web www.iforgetmetm.com

www.tabithamcclarity.com

www.ingramcontent.com/pod-product-compliance
Lightning Source LLC
Chambersburg PA
CBHW021219090426
42740CB00006B/288
9781733442602